the CUB SCOUT

annual 1982

The Official Cub Scout Annual

Edited by David Harwood

THE COVER PHOTOGRAPHS

Front

A dream come true! A Cub Scout sits in the cockpit of a Formula 1 racing car. It all happened when three Cub Scouts went to see the Essex Lotus car being built. You can read about their exciting day inside.

photograph by David Stower

Back

For another special feature, three Cub Scouts went to the Headquarters of Ordnance Survey in Southampton to find out how maps are made. One of the instruments they saw — and tried out for themselves — was a Geodimeter mounted on a theodolite . . . what are they? Look at the feature on The Map Makers!

photograph by David Stower

A third special feature in this year's Annual is about how ropes are made. In this picture the Cubs are sitting in the stores of Bridon Fibres and Plastics.

photograph by Harold Wyld.

This Annual belongs to:

CROSSWORD Test Your KnOWLedge

Devised and Illustrated by Ann Pinder

CLUES DOWN

2. Insects, worms, mice and, in the breeding season, birds are all _ _ _ _ of the Little Owl (4)
3. The _ _ _ _ eared Owl is named for the tufts of feathers on its head, which are not ears even though they may resemble them (4)
4. Because of its white plumage, the Barn Owl is sometimes mistaken for one by startled people (5)
5. Species, not found in Britain, which preys on large birds and on animals the size of roe deer (5, 3)
6. The _ _ _ _ y Owl is a ground nesting species (4)
9. A nervous Little Owl will do this (3)
11. A country within the United Kingdom in which the Little Owl is found (5)
13. The famous bird photographer, Eric Hosking, lost one when photographing owls (3)
14. Popular nesting place for owls (4)
15. Owl claws (6)
17. The Snowy Owl may go _ _ _ _ _ _ _ for its food (7)
19. It is chiefly the female owl which will _ _ _ on the eggs to incubate them (3)
20. Owls have a reputation for being wise because the Little Owl was once sacred to this Greek goddess of wisdom (6)
23. Owls often _ _ _ _ _ _ _ their food whole (7)
25. This contains fur, feathers and bones, in fact all the food remains an owl cannot digest (6)
28. Part of Britain visited by the Snowy Owl (8)
30. A member of the crow family whose nest may be taken over and used by the Long-eared Owl (6)
34. An adult owl would not make an ideal one, particularly in the breeding season when it is very aggressive and protective towards its nest and territory (3)
36. See 38 Across.

CLUES ACROSS

1. The long, soft feathers at an owl's wing _ _ _ _ enable it to fly silently, an invaluable asset for a bird of prey (4)
3. An owl has two of these! (4)
6. The number of eggs in a Barn Owl's nest — a large clutch (5)
7. The number of months owl eggs are incubated for — though for owls that nest on the ground the period is shorter (3)
8. Another name for the Brown Owl (5)
10. The Little Owl sometimes rears _ _ _ broods annually (3)
12. The colour of the Little Owl's eyes (6)
14. Owl noise (4)
16. Small birds will do this to an owl in order to frighten it away (3)
18. The owl is a powerful, silent one (5)
19. Little Owls may be found beside the _ _ _ as they sometimes nest on coastal cliffs (3)
21. The colour of owl eggs (5)
22. An owl's _ _ _ _ fans out in flight (4)
23. Owls are not renowned as _ _ _ _ birds (4)
24. A small insectivore sometimes taken as prey — though not all owls will eat it as it has a bitter taste (5)
25. Owl beaks can give nasty ones (5)
26. The larger of a pair of owls (3)
27. Each owl's _ _ _ _ is curved and sharp (4)
29. Creature preyed upon by the Snowy Owl (7)
31. The _ _ _ _ mouse is widely eaten by owls (4)
32. Owls cannot digest this (4)
33. An owl gets a firm _ _ _ _ on its prey (4)
35. It is illegal to do this to owls (4)
37. The time when most owls are about (5)
38 & 36 Down. Short-eared Owls may be seen in _ _ _ _ _ _ GLIA (4, 2)
39. A young Long-eared Owl makes a whining noise like this animal (3)

Check your answers on page 63.

Most of you will know that our Founder, Robert Baden-Powell, was a soldier before he started Scouting. He had an outstanding military career, but the one event for which he is particularly remembered is the Siege of Mafeking during the Boer War in South Africa at the turn of the century.

In October 1899, B.-P. took 1,000 men to the small, but strategically important town of Mafeking. The Boers marched on Mafeking with 9,000 men and surrounded it. Everyone expected it to be taken, but it held out for 218 days until it was relieved. The siege caught the imagination of England. When news of the relief of Mafeking reached Britain, the whole country celebrated, and B.-P. became the nation's hero.

In this feature, Garnie Muller (who is Chairman of the Mafeking Boy Scout-Girl Guide Committee) imagines he is . . .

The 100th day of the siege, and Mafeking's Town Guard gather for prayers.

A Wolf Cub in Mafeking

Akela tells us that we are lucky to be living in the small town of Mafeking in the northern part of the Cape Province in the Republic of South Africa. She says that this is the place where a man called Baden-Powell got the idea of Boy Scouts a long time ago, even before my grandfather was born. I know that great-grandfather was here as we have a big cannon shell which we use as a door stop in our home that was fired by the Boer people into Mafeking when great-grandfather was about my age and when, in 1899, Baden-Powell was sent by the British Government to defend Mafeking against the Boer forces.

I know what great-grandfather looked like, as I've seen his picture taken with a lot of other boys who were called the Siege Cadets. My Dad says that there was a war and the Boers were all around the town and they used to shoot the big shells into Mafeking, but they did not do a great deal of damage as most of the houses were made of clay bricks and the shells went right through them.

The schools were closed because of the siege and the boys became a bit naughty as they had nothing to do all day. A man called Lord Edward Cecil decided to do something with these boys. He was a busy man as he

Lord Edward Cecil, who formed and trained the Mafeking Siege Cadet Corps.

Photographs by courtesy of the Mafeking Museum.

1. B.-P. sketching on the verandah of lawyer Minchin's office, which he had comandeered for his use.

2. B.-P. on the roof of Minchin's building.

3. An orderly sounding the alarm with his bugle to warn the Town Guard to get into the trenches as the Boers were advancing. Note the Cadet on the bicycle, the ambulance wagon close to the tree, and B.-P.'s look-out on the top of Minchin's building (arrowed).

4. An armoured train used in Mafeking during the siege.

5. Cannon Kopje, B.-P.'s main fort during the siege.

assisted Baden-Powell. With Baden-Powell's permission, he taught the boys how to drill and to march and named them the Mafeking Siege Cadet Corps. Soon the lads were doing a great job of work, their main task being carrying messages within the town. At first they used donkeys when they had to go to a far-off place, but later — when the food in Mafeking became very short — the poor donkeys had to be slaughtered to feed the besieged inhabitants.

Fortunately a big store in the town had a number of bicycles in stock which Lord Cecil managed to acquire to replace the donkeys. The Cadets found the bikes much better than the donkeys as they could race around so much faster, especially when the town was being shelled.

I've seen a very old postage stamp that was made in Mafeking because the Post Office had run out of stamps and could not get any more because the town was cut off. The stamp shows a boy called Warner Goodyear, who was the head boy, with his bike. The Siege Cadets looked quite smart in the uniforms which Lord Cecil managed to get from the big store, a khaki tunic with long trousers and a small cap, which did not fit very well as some of the uniforms had to be cut down to more or less fit the boys.

Our Pack recently helped to restore the grave of Frankie Brown, the only Siege Cadet who died after his back was injured by pieces of a Boer shell.

The Pack has been on picnics to an old fort just outside Mafeking called Cannon Kopje. In South Africa we all speak two languages and Kopje means a small hill in the older form of the Afrikaans language. At Cannon Kopje we love to explore the old dug-outs and search for pieces of shells. A little while ago we dug up a very old and very rusty tent peg. Akela says that the peg was probably driven into the hard ground many, many years ago by a British soldier. Akela told us that Baden-Powell used Cannon Kopje as his main fort when defending the town because, from its elevated position, he could see the Boer guns and which way the barrels were pointing so he knew where they were going to fire and could quickly send a message to the people in the town.

Lord Edward Cecil telling amusing stories outside the staff dug-out. The officers (from left to right) are Captain Ryan; B.-P.; Lord Edward Cecil; Major Hanbury-Tracey; Captain Wilson; Lieutenant McKensie (sitting). Note the Cadet on either side.

The Postmaster, Mr. Howat, and Cadet Warner Goodyear beside the Post Office dug-out.

We have a very nice Mafeking District badge which we wear on our uniforms. It shows a pile of stones with a Scout hat. We chose the stones as, before the white people came here, the black people called the town Mafikeng, which means 'the place of stones' in their language.

The Mafeking District badge.

Although Baden-Powell was in Mafeking a long, long time ago, we Cubs know quite a lot about him as we have so many old photographs, and every few months we are finding out more and more as old papers are discovered. Akela says that we must remember that *we walk where B.-P. walked.*

Sunflower Power

by Ann Pinder

Illustrated by Melvyn Powell

The sunflower is a fascinating plant, and a useful one, too. In some countries, notably the USSR, India and Egypt, it is grown as a crop in the same way as wheat, barley and other cereals are grown in other parts of the world. All parts of the sunflower are useful to man. The stalks provide fuel for fires, the petals produce yellow dye and the leaves are given to animals as fodder. As for the seeds, these yield a sweet oil which is not only used in making margarine, paint and soap, but in Zimbabwe, when mixed with an equal quantity of diesel oil, it has even been tried as fuel for tractors and trucks.

In Britain, sunflower pictures appear on margarine packets, but in the USA it is seen in a much more exalted position — on the flag of Kansas. Kansas is often known as 'The Sunflower State' because so many of these plants are grown on the hot, sunny plains. Although Europe may not have the same climate as Kansas, sunflowers still do well in British gardens.

A year or two ago Cub Scout Simon Lambert raised over £17 for SHELTER (the National Campaign for the Homeless) with his 9 foot 1 inch sunflower.

photo: Worksop Guardian

Watch your funds grow with a SPONSORED SUNFLOWER GROW-IN . . .

If you are short of ideas for fund raising, why not try a sponsored sunflower grow-in? All you have to do is to get your family and friends to sponsor you a penny or 2p for each centimetre (or inch) of growth.

Being large sturdy plants, sunflowers are easy to grow... and they do grow at a terrific rate, sometimes reaching ten feet — or more — in height. Planted outdoors in May, in a sunny position, they bloom from July onwards, but they will bloom earlier if the seeds are germinated indoors in peat pots, and then transplanted outside in mid-May. Once your plants are in bloom, watch how each flower turns to follow the direction of the sun. It's at this stage that you should measure your prize sunflower, for once the flower fades, it soon droops.

Your Pack may decide to uproot its plants and bring them all to your Headquarters for measuring, but you can measure them all at home so the plants remain undisturbed.

As sunflowers are annuals, they do not bloom again the following year, but in the autumn each flowerhead will produce a large quantity of black and white striped seeds which garden birds — particularly greenfinches — will relish, giving you something new to watch in the garden once the summer and the sunflower season have passed.

THIS IS BUCKINGHAM PALACE

When the Royal Standard is flying from the main flag pole above the famous balcony on which the Royal Family make their appearances, it means that the Queen is actually in residence.

One of London's biggest tourist attractions is Buckingham Palace. Every day many people watch the ceremony of the Changing of the Guard, while others have it on their list of 'things to do'. If there's a special occasion and a chance of catching a glimpse of the Queen or a member of her family, crowds of people throng around the railings. For most people the view they get of the Palace is like the one shown in our photograph.

However, Buckingham Palace is the headquarters as well as the home of Her Majesty the Queen, who is the United Kingdom's Head of State. The Palace has about 600 rooms, but only a few of them are for the private use of the Royal Family. The rest are State Rooms, suites for official visitors, offices, domestic quarters, etc.

What's it like *inside* Buckingham Palace? Turn over the page and you'll get a bird's eye view!

photographs by David Stower

A bird's eye view of BUCKINGHAM PALACE

drawn by L. E. FANTAN

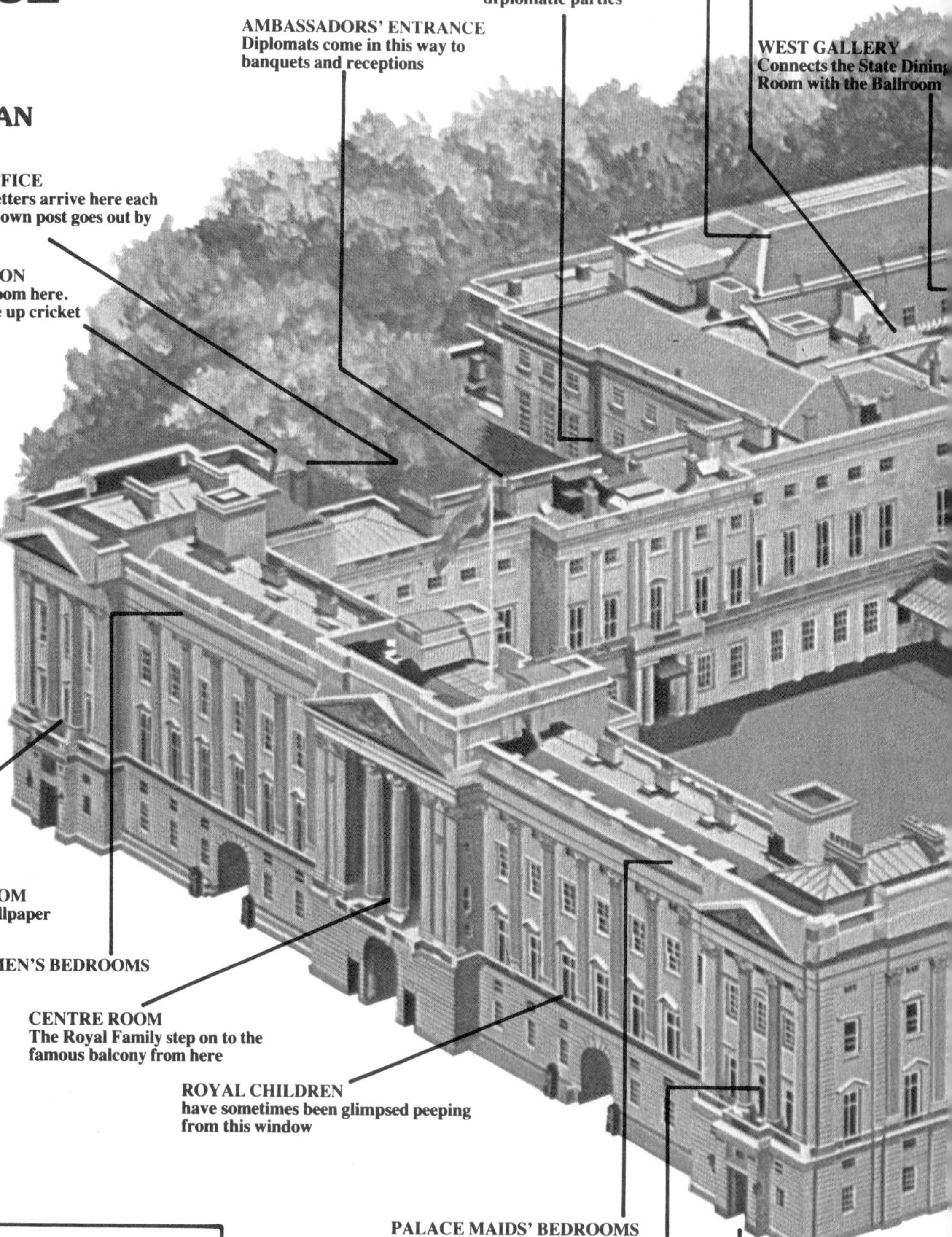

BALLROOM
Largest room in the Palace; state balls, banquets and investitures take place her

EAST GALLERY
A long room which leads fr the central block to the West Wing

WEST GALLERY
Connects the State Dinin Room with the Ballroom

STATE SUPPER ROOM
Sometimes used for diplomatic parties

AMBASSADORS' ENTRANCE
Diplomats come in this way to banquets and receptions

ROYAL POST OFFICE
Well over 50,000 letters arrive here each year. The Queen's own post goes out by registered mail

SERVANTS' RECREATION
They have a table tennis room here. (The staff sometimes make up cricket and golf sides, too.)

YELLOW DRAWING ROOM
has 18th-century yellow wallpaper

PALACE FOOTMEN'S BEDROOMS

CENTRE ROOM
The Royal Family step on to the famous balcony from here

ROYAL CHILDREN
have sometimes been glimpsed peeping from this window

PALACE MAIDS' BEDROOMS

CHINESE LUNCHEON ROOM
The Royal Family's private dining room is a long way from the kitchens. Before electricity, meals often went cold en route

PRIVY PURSE DOOR
Members of the public wishing to sign the book enter this way

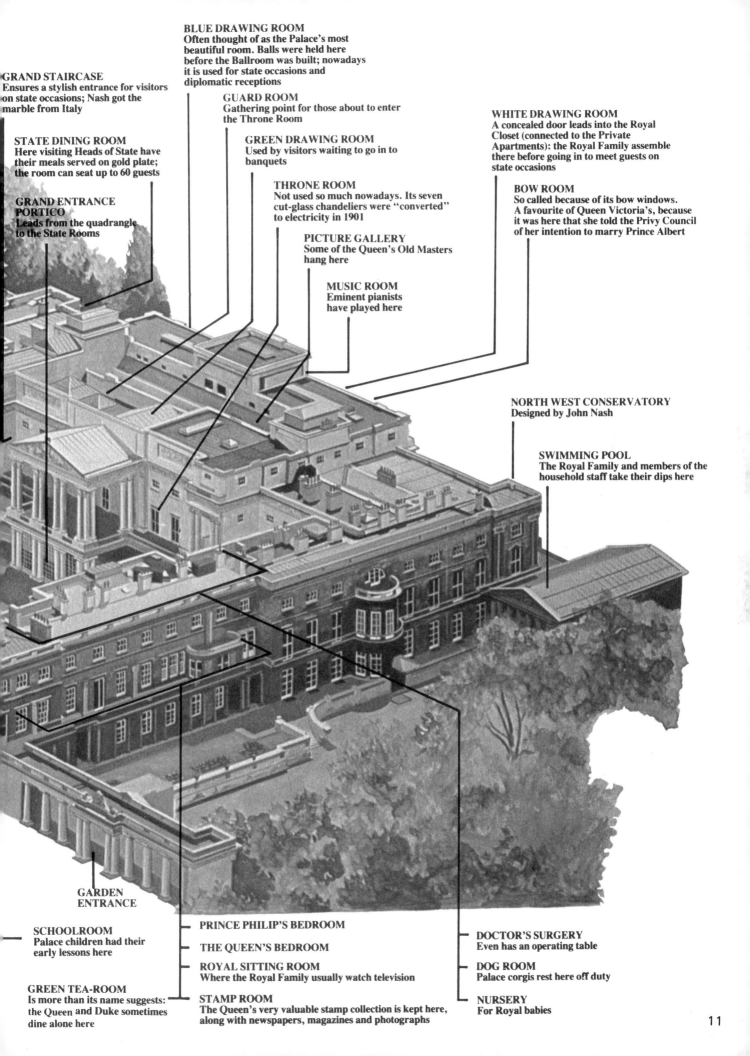

GRAND STAIRCASE
Ensures a stylish entrance for visitors on state occasions; Nash got the marble from Italy

STATE DINING ROOM
Here visiting Heads of State have their meals served on gold plate; the room can seat up to 60 guests

GRAND ENTRANCE PORTICO
Leads from the quadrangle to the State Rooms

BLUE DRAWING ROOM
Often thought of as the Palace's most beautiful room. Balls were held here before the Ballroom was built; nowadays it is used for state occasions and diplomatic receptions

GUARD ROOM
Gathering point for those about to enter the Throne Room

GREEN DRAWING ROOM
Used by visitors waiting to go in to banquets

THRONE ROOM
Not used so much nowadays. Its seven cut-glass chandeliers were "converted" to electricity in 1901

PICTURE GALLERY
Some of the Queen's Old Masters hang here

MUSIC ROOM
Eminent pianists have played here

WHITE DRAWING ROOM
A concealed door leads into the Royal Closet (connected to the Private Apartments): the Royal Family assemble there before going in to meet guests on state occasions

BOW ROOM
So called because of its bow windows. A favourite of Queen Victoria's, because it was here that she told the Privy Council of her intention to marry Prince Albert

NORTH WEST CONSERVATORY
Designed by John Nash

SWIMMING POOL
The Royal Family and members of the household staff take their dips here

GARDEN ENTRANCE

SCHOOLROOM
Palace children had their early lessons here

GREEN TEA-ROOM
Is more than its name suggests: the Queen and Duke sometimes dine alone here

PRINCE PHILIP'S BEDROOM

THE QUEEN'S BEDROOM

ROYAL SITTING ROOM
Where the Royal Family usually watch television

STAMP ROOM
The Queen's very valuable stamp collection is kept here, along with newspapers, magazines and photographs

DOCTOR'S SURGERY
Even has an operating table

DOG ROOM
Palace corgis rest here off duty

NURSERY
For Royal babies

11

THE NEST BOX CUBS

written and photographed by Michael Edwards

Success! A pair of blue tits found the Cubs' cherry wood box and made their nest inside. Here is one of them.

Stephen Porter sawed off a one-inch slice from the top of the log. This slice would be the lid of the box.

Using a 2" bit drill, a hole was drilled down the centre. Stephen Turner then chiselled out more wood while Margaret Allison lent a hand, as it is always important to have an adult present when using sharp tools. Stephen took care not to make the hole too big and left at least half an inch of wood all round for the wall.

Three Cub Scouts from the Leyland (St. James's) Pack in Lancashire discovered that working for their Handyman Proficiency Badge was a memorable and enjoyable experience.

During the winter months the boys had been feeding peanuts and seeds to blue tits and spent many happy hours observing the birds' acrobatic antics. The Cubs thought it would be a good idea to have the birds in the garden during the spring and summer and decided to make their feathered friends a nest box, particularly when they found out that there was a shortage of natural nest sites for hole-nesting birds.

What should their box be like? How would they make it? Rather than having a plywood box, the boys decided that a box which looked natural would be more attractive to the birds. Their Assistant Cub Scout Leader, Margaret Allison, provided a log of cherry wood, and they set to work. The photographs show how (with some help) they completed the task — *you* could make one, too!

The finished box was put in

position in February. It was fixed five feet off the ground in an apple tree, facing East because the birds like to greet the morning sun. It was protected by branches which, when in leaf, would help to hide the box.

The Cubs entered the first paragraph in their notebook on March 2nd, when a blue tit was seen inspecting the entrance hole. Two days later it went inside. A fortnight passed without any activity. Then two blue tits were spotted popping in and out.

The boys inspected the box on April 12th and found the beginnings of a nest. A week later they watched as the birds took hairs and the odd feather into the box. The first of eight brown speckled eggs was laid on April 22nd. Fourteen days later they hatched, and the parent birds were kept very busy fetching insects to feed their new family.

During their observations, the Cubs timed the parent blue tits. They noted that a parent returned to the chicks every two minutes with food, which was usually small caterpillars. Nineteen days after hatching, the young birds left their nest, fully feathered miniatures of their parents.

The Cubs are now waiting for next spring, to see if the birds will return — I'm sure they will!

Philip Balden screwed on the lid of the box with only one screw, which enabled the top to swivel to permit inspection.

Stephen Turner drilled the entrance hole. The size of the hole is very important. For blue tits its diameter should be 1¼". If the hole is too big, sparrows can get in.

Two coats of matt varnish were applied to the outside of the log. When dry, a wire loop was fixed to the back of the box with two staples.

A piece of ¾" timber, approximately the width of the box and as deep, was screwed to an apple tree. This 'back plate' would prevent water running down the trunk into the box. Finally, a nail was driven into the 'back plate' — but not driven home. The box was then hung onto the nail with the wire loop at the back of the box.

WILDLIFE IN CAMOUFLAGE 1

written and illustrated by Peter Harrison

Many animals have evolved ingenious ways of disguising themselves to enable them to hide from their enemies or to prey on others.
These pages show you some . . .

THE PTARMIGAN changes its plumage according to the season of the year.

THE HERMIT CRAB carries its home on its back and hides away when it senses there's danger about.

THE GRASS SNAKE sometimes pretends to be dead, which is one of the ways it protects itself from its enemies.

THE STOAT in its winter and its summer coat.

Some harmless insects imitate unpleasant species like the WASP to make other creatures imagine they are more harmful than they really are.

HOVER FLY

WASP BEETLE

HORNET MOTH

WASP

1. THE LAPPET MOTH merging with a background of dead leaves.
2. THE PHEASANT's plumage helps it to hide in a pile of autumn leaves.
3. THE LONG HORNED GRASSHOPPER resembles a partially dead leaf.
4. This CRAB is well hidden among a mass of seaweed.
5. A STICK INSECT looks just like a dead stick.

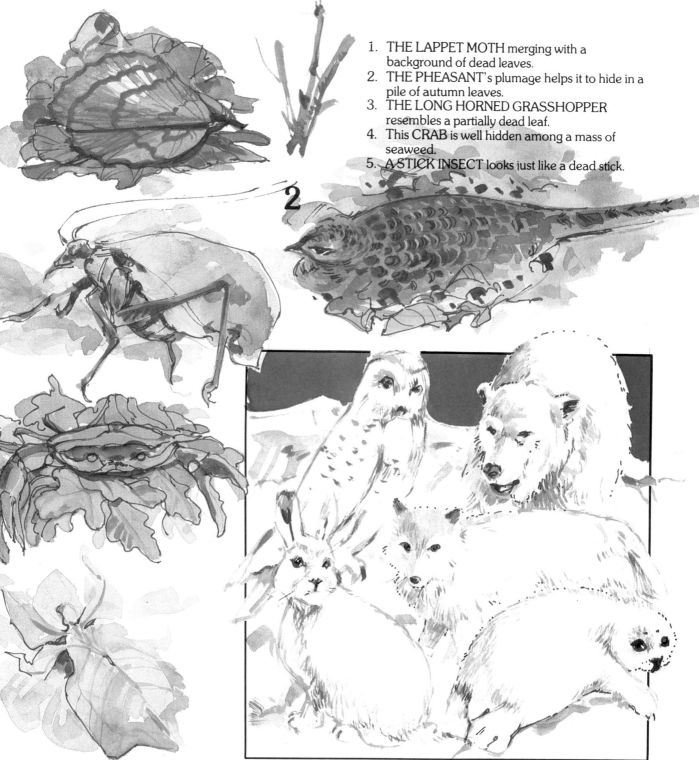

THE SNOWSHOE HARE, SNOWY OWL, POLAR BEAR, ARCTIC FOX and SEAL PUP all live in Arctic conditions, merging into their white habitat.

THE CABBAGE MOTH is dull coloured and well camouflaged.

Most FROGS and TOADS live on the ground and are coloured in shades of green and brown, helping them to hide in the mud and vegetation in which they live.

There's more Wildlife in Camouflage on pages 32 and 33.

Knots that ruled an Empire

by Eric Franklin

Illustrated by Peter Harrison

At one time a huge empire was ruled through the medium of knots, so there's no mistake in the title of this feature. This was the empire of the Incas of Peru, an empire which lasted for thirteen generations and stretched from the plains of the River Amazon to the Pacific Ocean. The Incas themselves were a comparatively small race but a race which, through superior ability and a genius for ruling, brought all the peoples around them into a union of one government.

The Incas ruled absolutely over a very mixed system of small states which, one after another, were brought to submission. They endured wars, devised social laws to benefit the various peoples, introduced land reforms, constructed canals and bridges, built fantastic temples and developed the various arts. In spite of all this, the Incas never developed the art of writing — they did everything without a written language, not even a form of picture writing like the Egyptians or the Chinese. What they had instead were knotted cords known as 'quipus'.

The quipus were not a substitute for writing, as the knots did not represent letters of the alphabet or words, but numbers. The Incas made the quipus into one of the cleverest recording and communicating devices the world has ever known. With these knotted ropes they kept records of everything that went on in their vast empire. The quipus were used to send messages; keep records of crops, tools, buildings and all sorts of accounts; take a census; and record nearly everything that everybody did from day to day and year to year.

Each quipu had a main horizontal cord, the length of which determined the particular purpose. A number of 'tied-on' cords, called depending cords, hung down from the main cord, rather like clothes on a washing line. The number of cords varied from a few to a hundred or more.

Vivid Colours

The ropes were made mainly from cotton and wool. They were woven by expert Peruvian ropemakers. They were so well made, and often dyed in vivid colours with natural vegetable dyes, that many have been found in Inca tombs and other places. This has meant that scientists and researchers today have been able to unravel at least a part of their fascinating story.

With the depending cords, the Incas evolved a decimal system using knots counted in rows starting at the bottom of the cord. A single overhand knot at the bottom was 'one'; in the next row up it stood for 'ten', in the third row for 'one hundred' and so on. To arrive at the other numbers, the knots had two, three, four turns and so on, the knots being what today we would call Blood Knots. The illustration shows the series of knots representing 1 to 9, the method of tying, and also an imaginary quipu.

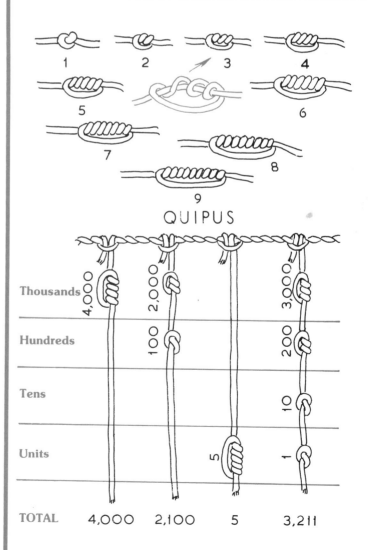

QUIPUS

	Thousands	Hundreds	Tens	Units
	4,000			
	2,000	100		5
	3,000	200	10	1
TOTAL	4,000	2,100	5	3,211

17

Knots that ruled an Empire
(continued)

Cords dyed in different colours were used to represent the past (i.e. events already happened) or the future (events due to occur either naturally or by decree). Other colours stood for specific things, e.g. metals such as gold or silver, grain or root crops, etc. Times of disaster, like floods or severe tempests, could be indicated by tying on additional coloured strands, while historical dates, astronomical calculations and other large numbers could be preserved.

Reports

Apart from the nationally kept quipus, individuals would keep their private accounts, perhaps as evidence for the tax-collector. Judges and magistrates used to send their reports to their superiors, showing sentences passed, the number of cases tried and what punishment had been given.

Every Inca village had accountants who recorded all events with knots — small villages had two or three (they also had to check each other) and the larger villages had perhaps twenty or more. These accountants kept records of births and deaths, the number of sheep and cattle, the production of wool and cloth, the battles fought and the numbers of people killed or injured and so on. All these knot records had to be sent from outlying villages to central places and eventually to the Inca capital so that the rulers had complete information throughout the entire empire.

Major Routes

The system used for these communications was also amazingly organized. The Incas built what we would now call trunk roads, which connected the capital with all major parts of the empire with lesser roads branching everywhere else. On all the major routes there were small block houses about five miles apart, and a number of trained runners were kept at each post ready to carry quipus back and forth: they were also trained to remember and carry any neccessary verbal explanatory messages, i.e. anything which couldn't be told by the knots. Their speed was such that they could carry their quipus in relays for up to 150 miles in one day.

Each district had officially appointed quipu keepers, known as 'Quipucamayus'. It was their job to collate information, marry together various quipus and keep the government informed on such matters as revenue, taxes, raw materials, food supplies and so on. There were also historians who knotted records to keep account of important events which, in this case, were more like the knots we tie in our handkerchiefs: they acted as memory aids to the verbal histories and legends which were passed down from father to son.

The comparatively little we know about quipus has come to us from the priests and scholars who followed the Spanish conquest of South America in the sixteenth century, together with the many examples which have been found in excellent preservation. The stories they tell, alas, are still held by the dead fingers of those who lived and tied their quipus centuries ago.

The Noble Order of St. John

by Raynor Evans

Perhaps at a football match or a pop concert, you may have seen the St. John Ambulance men in their black uniforms with the white bands round their hats, bearing a badge like the one in the picture. We get used to seeing them standing ready to give first aid and help wherever they are needed, so we tend to forget that they belong to a very noble Order going back for centuries.

At the time of the Crusades, when Richard the Lionheart was setting off for Jerusalem, a group of very wealthy and high-born Knights from various European countries banded together to try to help the Crusaders who came to defend the Holy Places, among them the Church of the Holy Sepulchre in Jerusalem.

Pilgrims to the Holy Land often arrived completely exhausted and dying of starvation. The journey to Jerusalem was long and, in those days, very difficult. Pilgrims had to fight bandits on the way, who robbed them of all their possessions. They were badly in need of rest and care before they were fit to travel on.

They found shelter in a hospice which had been established in the year 600 A.D., and rebuilt and enlarged 200 years later by the Emperor Charlemagne. But the mad Caliph El Hakim, who hated all Christians, destroyed the Church of the Holy Sepulchre together with the hospice. The pilgrims then had nowhere to shelter and were in a very sorry state.

A St. John Ambulance volunteer comforting an old person in distress.

photo: Chatham News Series

However after the death of the cruel Caliph, a group of merchants from Amalfi, in Italy, built a new hospital and church, and dedicated it to St. John the Baptist. In 1099, the Crusaders eventually captured Jerusalem after a bitter Holy War, and the victorious Knights were grateful for the rest and care given there which helped to heal their wounds.

Returning to their homes throughout Europe, the Crusaders told of the wonderful care they had received. Many rich Knights gave generously to the Benedictine monks who ran the hospital and, as their fame and wealth grew, the monks formed themselves into the Order of Hospitallers. They took the emblem of the eight-pointed cross of Amalfi to wear on their black sleeveless cloaks. The Order of Hospitallers moved to the site of the ancient monastery of St. John the Baptist in Jerusalem, and St. John became the Order's patron saint.

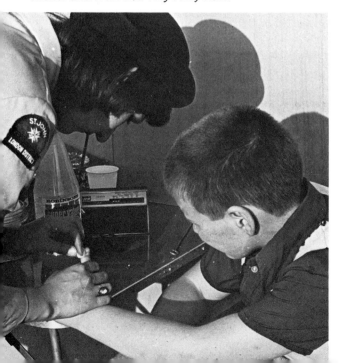

Many minor injuries — like this boy's cut thumb — are dealt with by St. John Ambulance volunteers on duty at a wide variety of outdoor entertainments and activities.

photo: Surrey Comet

Because the pilgrims continued to be attacked on the journey to Jerusalem, two French Knights decided to protect the pilgrims. Other Knights came to join them and the Order of Templars was formed.

The new Master of the Hospitallers, Raymond du Puy, was eager to give the Knights Templar, as the new military Order was known, as much support as possible. He took the bold step of suggesting that some of the Brothers at the hospital should take up arms and be ready to defend themselves if attacked, while still observing their vows of chastity, poverty and obedience.

The Brothers, many of whom came from noble families, were only too willing to fight, and many more fierce battles followed. This was continued for many years, the Moslems winning more and more ground, until finally Saladin, the Moslem Sultan, succeeded in conquering Jerusalem. The Hospitallers were forced to try and find a new refuge to carry on their work. Richard the Lionheart's recapture of the port of Acre gave them a chance to establish a hospital there for a time. So famous was the Order and its hospital that the city was known as St. Jean d'Acre.

Eventually Acre, too, fell to the Turks, and the Knights were forced to leave the Holy Land. They tried to settle on the island of Cyprus but were driven out, and finally took the island of Rhodes from the fierce Mediterranean pirates. Rhodes lies off the coast of Turkey in the Aegean Sea, and was an ideal half-way house for the Knights who hoped eventually to return to the Holy Land. They held Rhodes for 212 years during which the Order became richer, more powerful and able to defend itself against all comers.

However, the Knights were never left in peace. The Turks attacked and pressed them into battle. The ancient city of Rhodes was turned into a fortress. Great double walls rose sheer on the seaward side, and on the landward side there were two massive watchtowers separated by enormous dry moats. There were fortified watchtowers at every possible vantage-point so that the Knights could not be taken by surprise and, just to make things even more difficult for any invaders, the moats

A St. John Ambulance volunteer helps a holiday-maker who had been near to drowning off a beach. During the summer months St. John Ambulance have first aid posts at many popular resorts.

photo: Kentish Express

OUR CUB SCOUT LEADER HAD FORTY FITS!

IT WAS A LOVELY DAY WHEN OUR PACK WENT ON A SUPER NATURE TRAIL IN THE FOREST. AFTER COLLECTING A LOAD OF INTERESTING THINGS FOR FUTURE STUDY, AKELA DECIDED IT WAS TIME TO MAKE TRACKS FOR HOME.
"PACK! PACK! PACK!" HE YELLED.
"LET'S COUNT YOU–ONE–TWO–THREE–FOUR– YIKES! IS THAT ALL? THERE WERE TWENTY WHEN WE STARTED!" THE OTHER SIXTEEN THOUGHT THEY'D HAVE A LARK AND GO INTO HIDING. *CAN YOU FIND THEM?*

Argentinian soccer star Ossie Ardiles being carried off with a sprained ankle while playing for Tottenham Hotspur in September 1979.

photo:
Press Association

were inhabited by the poisonous snakes with which the island was infested. It is said that there are still snakes on Rhodes to this day and that is why the farmers wear high boots when working in the fields.

And so generation after generation of Knights under different Grand Masters fought terrible battles and died for the cause, but they always managed to hold on to the island, even withstanding a siege in 1480.

But finally, Suleiman, Sultan of Turkey, already a mighty warrior at the age of 29, turned his attention to the island in 1522. He was a sworn enemy of Christendom and was determined that he would not give in until he had conquered Rhodes. It took him six

months — this siege was more gruelling than the last in 1480 and was one of the most savage in history.

The Grand Master of the Order at that time was a noble Knight named Philippe de L'Isle Adam, a fine commander and Suleiman's equal in courage. The Knights fought magnificently, although they were greatly outnumbered. Even when there was hardly anything left to eat in the fortress and all the ammunition had been used, they refused to surrender. It was only when Suleiman sent a message threatening to slaughter the innocent islanders living outside the walls if the Knights did not hand over the fortress that they agreed to leave.

Continued on next page

Suleiman was so impressed by the valour of the Knights that he allowed them to take to their ships still carrying their swords — a great honour — and then he saluted his gallant adversary, L'Isle Adam.

However, the defeat successfully put an end to the Crusades, because the journey to Jerusalem was too difficult to make without the help of the Order. The Knights spent many years moving about from one place to another but never finding a permanent home until, in 1530, the Emperor Charles V of Spain presented the island of Malta to the Knights, on condition that they also defend Tripoli, in North Africa.

True to their vows, the very first thing they did was to build a hospital and each Knight, however high-born, was expected to tend the sick and do the most menial tasks. It is said that the Grand Master would himself go down on one day each week to the hospital and serve the patients' food and minister to their needs. The Knights always kept themselves fighting fit, as behoves every true Knight; there was always the danger of attack and they knew they must always be ready.

The attack came in 1565. Suleiman, now an old man of 71, had never forgotten the siege of Rhodes. He was furious that the Knights had found a new refuge and was determined to drive them out. He wanted the Mohammedan faith to be acknowledged as the true faith and vowed again to drive Christianity from the world.

Suleiman set out with the Turkish battle force of 30,000 men in 180 ships. The garrison of Malta comprised 541 Christian Knights, 5,000 Maltese militia and 3,000 other troops, including a picked body of Spanish infantry. The Maltese defenders were greatly outnumbered, but what they lacked in numbers they made up for in courage. The Grand Master at this time was a Frenchman named John de la Valette — also 71 years old — who was just as determined to fight for Christendom and to defeat the infidel.

The story of the battle that ensued has been handed from generation to generation and is one that Malta will never forget. This time the Knights refused to surrender and, in the end, it was the Turks who took to their ships, defeated. The town of Valetta, capital of Malta, was named after the indomitable hero, John de la Valette.

The Order has lived on in one form or another through the years, with the care of the sick and injured gradually becoming even more important as the fighting became unnecessary. Wherever war takes place, or disaster such as flood or earthquake strikes, the men and women of St. John Ambulance are always there. During the Second World War, many men became stretcher bearers and ambulance drivers with the fighting forces, while many more played their part in rescuing victims from bombed-out buildings during the Blitz.

Today, the men and women of St. John can be found wherever they are needed — wherever anyone could be injured or involved in an accident — at state occasions and processions, demonstrations, parades, fairgrounds, circuses, sitting at the back of theatres and on crowded beaches — always ready to give expert first aid.

And they still wear the eight-pointed cross of Amalfi, just as it was worn at the siege of Malta over four hundred years ago.

A daring cliff rescue by members of the St. John Ambulance in Guernsey, Channel Islands.

photo: Guernsey Press

Feather CROSSWORD

by Ann Pinder

CLUES ACROSS

2. This might make us cough, but birds stand in it deliberately to rid themselves of insect pests (5)
4. The crest of this bird resembles blades of grass — perfect camouflage when sitting on its nest (7)
7. Bright, migrant birds with feathers which look like red sealing wax (8)
9. Birds' feathers are coated with this substance to make them waterproof (3)
11. The Australian _ _ _ _ Bird's tail looks like an old-fashioned harp (4)
12. Duck with green and chestnut head. Found among the tea leaves? (4)
14. Scottish gamebird which turns white in Winter (9)
15. Woodland bird with bright blue wingbars (3)
16. The Gold_ _ _ _ _ is Britain's smallest bird, named for the yellow feathers on its head (5)
18. Member of the crow family which has a bald patch above its beak (4)
23 & 29. The down with which this bird lines its nest is collected for filling bedroom quilts (5, 4)
24. White feathers give this owl a ghostlike appearance (4)
25. Long-legged wader with drooping tail feathers. You might find one on a building site! (5)
27. Bird feathers are often used to line this (4)
30. This bird is sometimes called the 'sea swallow' because of its long forked tail (4)
32. Bird seen on lakes. One kind has a distinctive chestnut ruff (5)
33. Insects that preening birds encourage, since they squirt formic acid on to the birds' feathers, thereby dislodging parasites (4)

CLUES DOWN

1. British sea duck. The male is mainly white. The female has a red head (4)
3. Birds of _ _ _ _ _ _ _ _ have the most heavenly feathers of all (8)
5. How many other creatures — apart from birds — have feathers? (4)
6. Feather pen (5)
8. Garden bird with irridescent feathers (8)
10. Plumes from these birds once adorned hats and fans (9)
13. _ _ _mary. Name of long wing feathers (3)
14. Bird with a train full of eyes (7)
17. Small garden bird (3)
19. Bird of prey named for the shape of its tail. You might fly one of these on a string (4)
20. _ _ _wing. A member of the thrush family, only seen in Britain in winter (3)
21. A bird does this to keep its feathers in good condition (6)
22. Black_ _ _, a bird named for the black feathers on its head (3)
25. Bird partner, usually with more colourful feathers than its mate (4)
26. A bird does this at least once a year to renew its feathers (5)
28. Like other birds of prey these have well-feathered legs (6,
31. Red feathers have linked this bird with Christmas since the Christmas postman once wore a red coat (5)

Check your answers on page 63.

How the Tortoise got his shell

An Australian animal legend re-told

Illustrated by Martin Aitchison

FOLKLORE TELLS many splendid stories to explain the strangeness of certain animals, and here is one of the strangest — about the tortoise, and it comes from Australia.

It is said that long, long ago the birds and animals lived in a deep valley surrounded by high hills. Food was scarce, so a meeting was held and it was decided that the big eagle-hawk, the king of birds, should fly over the range to look for food.

Away flew the eagle-hawk until he came to a beautiful country full of food. There was no sign of any other animals or birds, except one little willy-wagtail, who said: 'If you come here for food, you must wrestle with me first.' But the strong eagle-hawk didn't know that the cunning little willy-wagtail had placed some sharp fish-bones like spikes in the ground. They began to wrestle, and the willy-wagtail tripped up the other bird, who fell among the spikes and was held there.

Then in turn the kite-hawk, the magpie, the wombat and the dingo travelled over the ranges to this new land, but the wicked willy-wagtail caught them all on his spikes, and none returned to the valley. The birds and animals became more and more alarmed, until at last the old tortoise volunteered to go.

He journeyed slowly but surely over the ranges and, as before, the willy-wagtail greeted him with his challenge. But the tortoise in his slow sure way thought about the matter first, and went into the bush where he carved a coolamon, which is a wooden dish, and cut a thick strip of bark from a gum tree. He placed the coolamon on his back and tied the thick bark as a breast-plate. Then he went to wrestle with the cunning willy-wagtail.

The lively little wagtail soon tripped up the slow old tortoise, just as he had the others, but the tortoise was saved from the spikes by his back and breast plates. On and on went the struggle, until at last the willy-wagtail became exhausted, and the tortoise won the fight.

With his wisdom and cunning the slow old tortoise succeeded where all the others had failed by the use of force. And that is why, so says the legend, the tortoise to this day carries the breast and back plates — as a memorial to his great victory.

THIS IS
Team Lotus!

THE CUB SCOUT ANNUAL FINDS OUT ABOUT THE BUILDING OF A GRAND PRIX RACING CAR

Words: David Harwood
Photographs: David Stower & LAT Photographic

You've probably watched Grand Prix motor racing on television. You may have been to a race meeting or even to the British Grand Prix. I wonder how many times you have imagined that you're the World Champion racing driver, following in the footsteps of such men as Jackie Stewart and Alan Jones? There's something thrilling and exciting about car racing, isn't there?

But the start of a Grand Prix is the end of months — often years — of hard work, skill, inventiveness and practice. As soon as one race is over, the cars have to be prepared, and possibly repaired, for the next. Each year new cars are designed and built, each competing team trying to do better than all the others.

Many CUB SCOUT ANNUAL readers asked for a feature on motor racing, so we decided to try and see the building of a racing car. We wrote to one of the British teams — Team Lotus — and were invited to take three Cubs to their Norfolk headquarters.

And so, in November 1979, Paul Adler of the 9th Pinner (Remus) Pack travelled north from London to Norwich with our photographer, David Stower. "As the train got closer to Norwich, I became more and more excited," Paul remembers. "We took a taxi from the station and were soon out in the country. I was most surprised when we turned a corner and arrived at an airfield beside which was a very modern factory where the Lotus production cars are made."

From the factory, Paul, Mr. Stower and I were taken by chauffeur-driven car along narrow, winding lanes. After a mile or two we turned off the road and up a long drive which led to Ketteringham Hall, a magnificent mansion set in its own estate. It was not the sort of place Paul expected to be the home base of a famous car racing team.

Paul met Christopher Flegg and Andrew Spiller from the local Wymondham Cub Scout Pack. We all went into the Hall, where we were welcomed by Mr. Glenn Waters, Team Lotus' Senior Mechanic. He told the boys that there were three main parts to the team — 'development' for introducing new designs and techniques; 'manufacturing' for actually making the racing cars, and 'racing' for getting the cars, equipment, mechanics and everything else around the world, not only for the Grand Prix races, but also for tests and practices.

Mr. Waters then took the boys on a guided tour of the Hall. The boys asked lots of questions . . .

THE PHOTOGRAPHS	
Top left:	Elio de Angelis at the wheel of the Lotus (Car No. 12) at the 1980 Monaco Grand Prix.
Top right:	Mario Andretti in Car No. 11 at the German Grand Prix 1980.
Bottom left:	Elio de Angelis at the 1980 South African Grand Prix.
Bottom right:	Mario Andretti in the Lotus cockpit at the 1980 German Grand Prix.

Designer Jerry Booen showing Paul, Andrew and Christopher a plan on which he was working in the drawing office.

The boys inspecting the wheels of the car . . . inside and out!

Glenn Waters explaining the workings of the Ford Cosworth engine.

The Cubs watched Fabrication Supervisor Roy Franks and Tony Fletcher fitting a piece to the front of the chassis of the 1980 car . . .

Do you build a completely new car each year?

No, but we are always making modifications and improvements. We are building a new one for next season (1980) and you'll see something of that shortly. The starting point for any development is an idea, and then that idea has to be designed, drawn, made and tested. This is what they're doing here in the drawing office. Much of the work here is secret, as we don't want our competitors to know what we're doing!

We moved on to a room with racks full of cog wheels lining the walls.

We build our own gear boxes here. The cogs in these racks are the various gear ratios which are fitted inside the gearbox casing.

How many gears does the car have?

Five forward gears plus reverse. A reverse gear is compelled by the regulations to assist in getting a car out of trouble if it spins on the track.

In the next room there were stacks of silver coloured objects, which were shaped somewhat like milk churns.

This is where the wheels are stored. They're made in Italy for us. We need quite a lot. For each Grand Prix we take about 120 for the two cars. Carry one outside and have a good look. Please don't drop them, as they cost about £350 each!

Do you make your own tyres?

No. Goodyear make them. They send a trailer with about 1,400 tyres to each Grand Prix.

What are the tyres like?

We have a number of different tyres. The important thing about any tyre is its grip. For racing, wet weather tyres do have treads to pump away the water, but a dry weather tyre is smooth and needs to be quite hot to grip effectively. That's why drivers appear to swerve on the track on the warm-up lap — they're warming up their tyres to get a good grip.

How do you know when a dry-weather tyre is wearing out of it doesn't have a tread?

There are a number of 'pits' in it, the depth of which indicate how much of the outer tyre is left.

How long will a set of tyres last?

If all goes well, they should last for 200 miles, which would be a full race. But all sorts of things can happen — there's a change in the weather half way through a race and the tyres have to be changed from wet to dry, or from dry to wet, and there's always the possibility of a puncture or a blowout.

... studied the chassis from every angle ...

... and inspected the cockpit thoroughly.

Two men were working at one end of the next workshop, but what caught the boys' attention first was a large engine resting on a cradle.

This is the engine which powers the car. It's a 3000 cc Ford Cosworth which, as you can see, has eight cylinders.

Does it need special fuel?

It runs on 5-star petrol, so it's not a lot different from the petrol your dad would put in his car.

How many miles to the gallon will it do?

Around 5.5 to 6 miles per gallon.

How many engines do you have?

Twenty-four. The racing team takes ten to each race. After a race, each engine used it stripped down and re-built.

How much do they cost?

About £23,000 each.

The boys made their way to the other end of the workshop, where two engineers were working on what appeared to be a large model car.

This is the chassis of one of the 1980 cars.

The moment of suprise as the boys took off the tarpaulin of the 1979 car.

Christopher, Paul and Andrew roll the car out into the courtyard.

Where do they get the bits to make the cars from?

They make them! Designers and draughtsmen make drawings — like the ones you saw in the drawing office — and each piece is then precision made down here.

What are the pieces made from?

Aluminium.

It doesn't look much like a racing car!

Not yet, no. But it will when the shell is fitted over it.

How many cars do you make?

Four — one for each of the two drivers, plus two spare ones. Each is exactly the same, except for the cockpit.

What's different about the cockpits?

The seats. Each seat is made to fit the individual driver. He sits on a kind of flexible bag into which plastic foam is injected. We can then make a mould which exactly matches the shape of his body.

Where does the petrol go?

In a flexible petrol tank. It's made out of a woven Kelvar cloth (called 'FT 3') which is coated with rubber on both sides. It's very tough.

Why is it flexible?

It's much less likely to burst if there's an accident.

How much petrol will it hold?

Forty gallons.

Continued on page 30

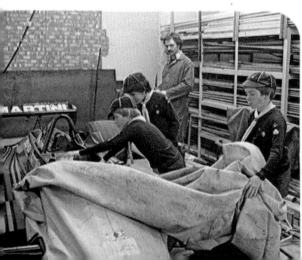

Cutaway drawing of the
ESSEX LOTUS EL81
drawn by Tony Matthews
reproduced by courtesy of Team Essex Lotus

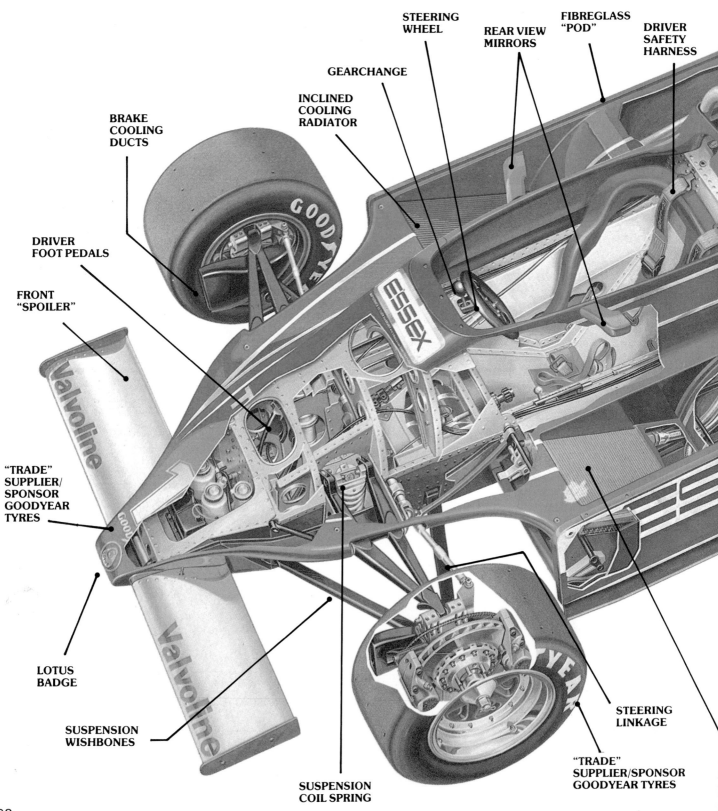

ROLL OVER BAR
FOR DRIVER
PROTECTION

STEERING
WHEEL

REAR VIEW
MIRRORS

FIBREGLASS
"POD"

DRIVER
SAFETY
HARNESS

GEARCHANGE

INCLINED
COOLING
RADIATOR

BRAKE
COOLING
DUCTS

DRIVER
FOOT PEDALS

FRONT
"SPOILER"

"TRADE"
SUPPLIER/
SPONSOR
GOODYEAR
TYRES

LOTUS
BADGE

SUSPENSION
WISHBONES

SUSPENSION
COIL SPRING

STEERING
LINKAGE

"TRADE"
SUPPLIER/SPONSOR
GOODYEAR TYRES

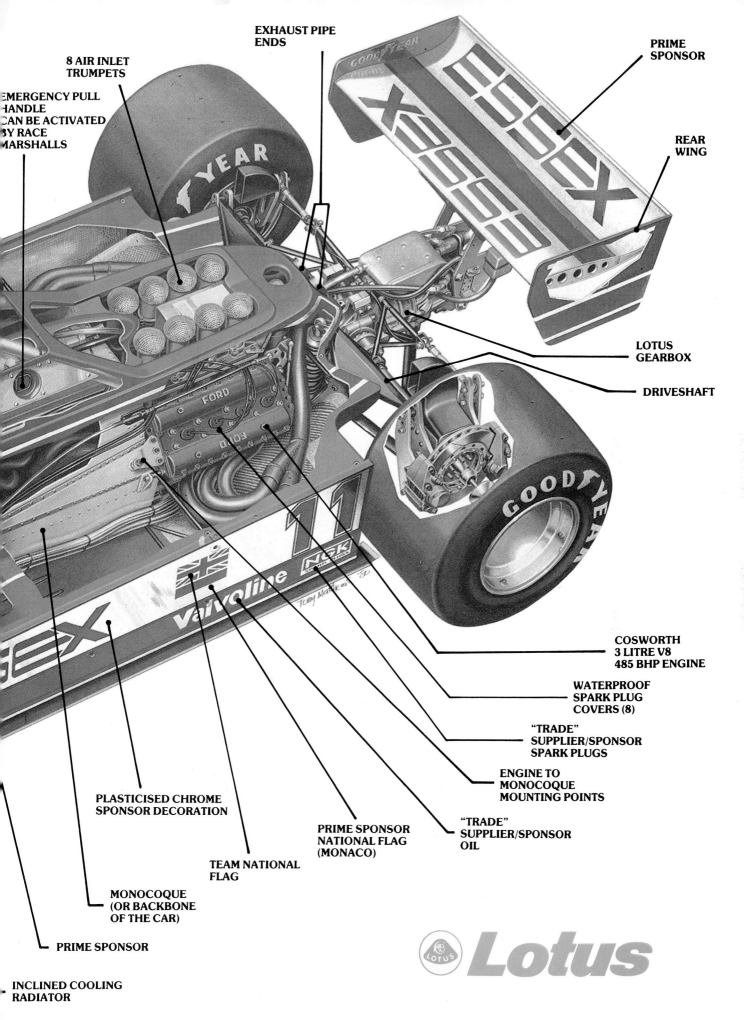

EXHAUST PIPE ENDS

8 AIR INLET TRUMPETS

PRIME SPONSOR

EMERGENCY PULL HANDLE CAN BE ACTIVATED BY RACE MARSHALLS

REAR WING

LOTUS GEARBOX

DRIVESHAFT

COSWORTH 3 LITRE V8 485 BHP ENGINE

WATERPROOF SPARK PLUG COVERS (8)

"TRADE" SUPPLIER/SPONSOR SPARK PLUGS

ENGINE TO MONOCOQUE MOUNTING POINTS

PLASTICISED CHROME SPONSOR DECORATION

PRIME SPONSOR NATIONAL FLAG (MONACO)

"TRADE" SUPPLIER/SPONSOR OIL

TEAM NATIONAL FLAG

MONOCOQUE (OR BACKBONE OF THE CAR)

PRIME SPONSOR

INCLINED COOLING RADIATOR

Lotus

The boys followed Glenn Waters through another workshop, a section of which was hidden from view by a curtain. The Cubs were curious to know what was behind it. Mr. Waters explained that it was a 'forbidden area' because the prototype of the shell of the 1980 car was there. "It's secret," he said. "We cannot allow anyone outside the team — not even you — to see it. But come along with me."

The Cubs walked down a passage into what had once been a stable. It was dark. Mr. Waters switched on the lights. There were racks along the walls, and something under a tarpaulin. At first the lads didn't seem to be particularly interested.

"Could you take off that tarpaulin, please?" Mr. Waters asked. The boys went to one end and started to remove the cover. They hadn't pulled back more than a foot or two before their faces lit up.

"Phew!"

"Hey! What's this?"

They couldn't believe their eyes, and the last part of the tarpaulin was removed more quickly than the first.

There, in all its shining livery, was a real racing car!

"This is the car Mario Andretti drove this season," Mr. Waters told them. "Would you like to have a good look at it?"

You can guess what the boys reaction was. The stable doors were opened, and the trio pushed the car into the courtyard. For the next half hour the Cubs not only inspected every part of the car — the ceramic skirts, the tyres, the aerofoil, the bodywork, and so on — but they also took it in turns to sit in the cockpit.

They looked at the instrument panel and noticed there was no speedometer: just a rev. counter, a fuel and oil pressure gauge, and a water and oil temperature gauge. One of them found the emergency knob which would cut the engine and set off the fire extinguishers in the event of an accident (no one actually pulled it!). They were amazed at how small the cockpit seemed to be, and remarked on the way the driver had to sit with his legs straight forward. Andrew commented on the smallness of the steering

wheel and discovered (by mistake!) that it would come off. Paul imagined that he was going round a circuit at the car's maximum speed of 180 miles an hour, while Christopher timed the 10 seconds it would take to reach 150 miles an hour from a standing start. All were surprised that the only protection the driver would have from the wind and the weather on his face was the visor on his crash helmet.

The Cubs helped to put the car away, and wondered why it had to be parked on a weighbridge. "That's because we have to make sure the car's weight is evenly distributed between the front and the back," Glenn Waters explained.

The visit was almost over. Before the boys said a final 'thank you', they were each given some mementos of their visit. While Andrew and Christopher had only to go a mile or two to Wymondham, Paul had a long journey back to London. He was very tired when he finally arrived home in Hatch End, Middlesex, but, as far as he was concerned, it had been the best day of his life.

The boys listen intently as Glenn Waters answers their questions.

Andrew discovered that the steering wheel will come off!

One last look! The boys have pushed the car back into the stable onto the weighbridge.

Paul in his element — note the ceramic skirt touching the ground between the wheels.

THE CUB SCOUT ANNUAL gratefully acknowledges the help of all concerned at Team Lotus without whose co-operation this feature would not have been possible.

flags at sea

Illustrated by Peter Stuckey

Flags have been used for communication for hundreds of years. In the 17th, 18th and 19th centuries a properly organised international code of naval signals gradually developed. Messages did not have to be spelled out letter by letter, and certain combinations of flags meant the same in several languages.

The latest code came into operation in 1969 and can be 'read' in English, French, German, Italian, Japanese, Spanish, Norwegian, Russian and Greek. While signal flags are still used for a few specialised purposes, they have been largely superceded by the radio telephone and the radio telegraph. However, flags are still used on important occasions when ships are 'dressed overall' (or rainbow fashion, as it is also called).

Sail training ship *Danmark* dressed overall.

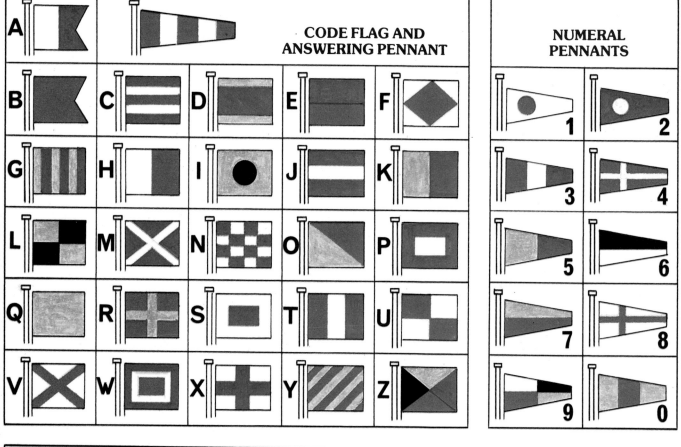

CODE FLAG AND ANSWERING PENNANT

NUMERAL PENNANTS

A B C D E F G H I J K L M N O P Q R S T U V W X Y Z

1 2 3 4 5 6 7 8 9 0

SUBSTITUTES   First   Second   Third

WILDLIFE IN CAMOUFLAGE 2

AT THE BOTTOM OF THE SEA

1. THE ANGEL SHARK rests on the sea bottom and lies in wait for its prey to swim by.
2. THE SPIDER CRAB looks like — and hides in — coral.
3. THE ANGLER FISH have bodies covered with a variety of warts and flaps of skin to make them look like rocks and seaweed. They have a 'fishing rod' fin suspended over their mouths from which they have taken their name.
4. THE OCTOPUS is a master of disguise, spending most of its time among rocks, where it changes its body colouring to match its surroundings.
5. The ugly STONEFISH closely resembles a rock and is most difficult to recognise when resting on the ocean floor.
6. THE SHRIMPFISH has the ability to stand on its head when danger is around and is so thin that it seems to disappear among the plant leaves.
7. THE PLAICE and TURBOT are flat fish which rest on the bottom of the sea, their skin looking like sand and small stones.
8. THE BLENNY's mottled colouring blends in with the rocks and the seaweed in which it lives.

THE BITTERN (right) is rarely seen and when alarmed it freezes like a statue, stretching its neck towards the sky.

written and illustrated by Peter Harrison

The American ALLIGATOR can easily be mistaken for a dead log on a river bank where it waits for animals to come and drink.

THE HEDGEHOG hides through the day in dried leaf litter and can roll itself up into a ball when danger threatens.

During the day, this TAWNY OWL has a favourite resting spot and is well hidden with its brown colours. It hunts at night for shrews, voles, mice and other small mammals.

THE TREECREEPER holds on to the bark of a tree where it searches for insects and grubs.

Is that a PANTHER silhouetted on the branch?

THE CHAMELEON can change its colour to suit its surroundings.

There are many more animals and insects which camouflage themselves. We've shown you a few — how many others do you know or can you discover?

THE MIRACLE OF TREES

by Nancy Scott

Illustrated by Peter Harrison

Would you like to see the miracle of the birth of a tree? You can, if you carry out this experiment carefully.

First, make a collection of *tree* seeds. You can begin with apple and pear pips, then by searching among the leaves beneath the trees in parks, gardens, woods and hedgerows, you should be able to find sycamore wings, ash and elm keys, hazel nuts, horse chestnuts, beech mast — all with their seeds still safely enclosed. You will find many cones still clinging firmly on pine and fir branches.

When you have as many different seeds as you can find, then take them home and plant them in a miniature greenhouse. This is how you make one of your own. You will need either a glass dish with a lid, or a plastic ice-cream container, or a plastic sandwich box, with a clear lid. On the bottom of your container place a flat wet sponge, and on this arrange your seeds. It will be better to nick the covering of the larger hard-skinned seeds in several places. This will allow the moisture to enter them more quickly and more effectively. You can do this nicking process with a nail file, as that is safer than using a knife or scissors.

Put the lid on the container, and stand it on a warm windowsill, where it will get all the sun possible. Now you must be patient, because tree seeds do not grow as quickly as cress seeds, with which you may already have experimented. And you must keep the sponge damp, too. How often it will need 'watering' will depend on the amount of sunshine — so you also need to observe the weather during this experiment.

In a while you will see the first signs of growth, and then you will see the actual birth of a tree. You will be able to watch how the roots form, and the beginning of the tiny trunk which will one day, if cared for, grow into a bark-covered tower of strength.

By the time each little tree is about two inches high, you should start transplanting them into pots of soil. Use paper pots of the type that will eventually dissolve in the soil — you can buy these very cheaply from a garden supply shop. The reason for using paper pots is that later on you will want to plant your little tree in the garden, or a friend's garden, and when that time comes you can put the tree *and the pot* straight into the soil, and so avoid damaging the root system.

Of course, if you want to grow a selection of miniature trees to keep on your window-sill, plant your seedlings in ordinary plastic plant pots, first putting a few stones at the bottom of the pot to help the drainage.

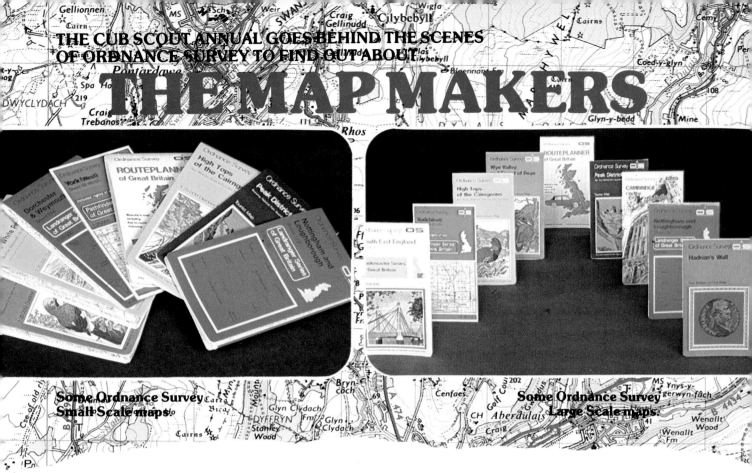

THE MAP MAKERS

Some Ordnance Survey Small Scale maps.

Some Ordnance Survey Large Scale maps.

THERE MUST BE few days when you don't see or use a map. They're so common nowadays that we tend to take them for granted. Maps are printed in books, newspapers and magazines; shown on television to indicate where something has happened or to help the weatherman give his forecast; displayed in town centres to enable people to find their way about. Maps are used by all sorts of people — planners, surveyors and engineers, concerned with new towns, roads, gas, electricity, water, oil and coal; solicitors and architects concerned with land and buildings; scientists, geologists, police, and 'ordinary' people going on journeys on foot, by bicycle and by car. All this illustrates the most important function of a map — it is useful, and meant to be used.

A number of organisations publish maps, but by far the largest in Great Britain is the Ordnance Survey, which is the country's official survey and map-making organisation. Each Ordnance Survey map contains a wealth of information. But where does the information come from? How does the information get onto a printed sheet of paper which you can buy from a shop in almost every town in the land? THE CUB SCOUT ANNUAL decided to find out . . .

Ordnance Survey Headquarters, Southampton.

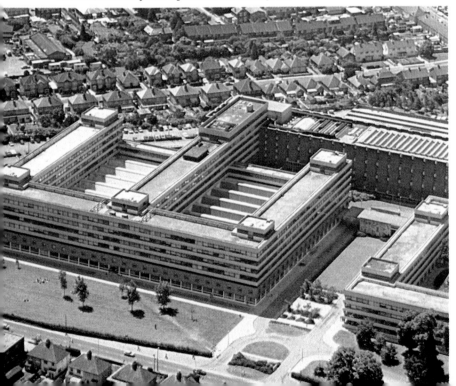

One day last summer three Cub Scouts travelled to the headquarters of Ordnance Survey at Maybush on the outskirts of Southampton. The boys were Richard Penny of the 6th North Watford (Beta) Pack; Mark Blackburn of the 11th Southampton (St Boniface) Pack; and Simon Harwood of the 1st Frampton Cotterell 'A' Pack. Their task was to get an idea of how maps are made, and their guide and host for the day was Mr. Richard Cameron, who is Ordnance Survey's Manager of Information and Public Relations.

words by David Harwood and Dick Cameron

photographs by David Stower

Mr. Cameron explaining the purpose of a Triangulation Station to Simon, Mark and Richard.

As the boys were to be surveyors for the first part of the day, each was kitted out with a fluorescent orange waistcoat and a yellow safety helmet. Then they climbed to the summit of a mound in the grounds of the huge complex.

"This is a 'Triangulation Station'," Mr. Cameron explained when the boys reached a concrete pillar. "It's one of a great many and is very important to the map maker. You see, to map a country you need to be able to measure horizontal angles and distances, and vertical angles and heights very accurately. You may have learnt at school that if you can measure the exact length of one side of a triangle, and can measure two of the three angles, you can calculate the lengths of the other two sides. This was the basic system which the Ordnance Survey

Richard looks thoughtfully at the theodolite 3 bar mounting bracket on the top of the pillar.

used when it was founded in 1791 to provide the British Army with accurate maps of the South coast of England. At that time there was a threat of war from — and possible invasion by — the French.

"The starting point was a 5 mile long straight 'base line' measured on Hounslow Heath (now London Airport). From each end of the line, those first surveyors measured the angle to a third point to make a triangle. Once they had a base triangle, they could make other triangles. Thus a network of triangles was built . . . each corner being marked as a 'Triangulation Station'. In those early days it may have been a wooden post or even the upended barrel of a cannon."

How many Stations are there today?
More than 25,000.

Are they all like this one?
No, there are only about 5,000 of these 4 foot high concrete pillars but they are the most obvious as they are usually placed on high and exposed places. The others might be church spires, or bolts set in church towers or tall buildings and lightning conductors on factory chimneys.

What are these 3 metal bars for?
They're the anchor points for a theodolite which a surveying team will mount on top of the pillar when they are taking measurements.

What's a theodolite?
It's an instrument for measuring horizontal and vertical angles. When the Ordnance Survey began its work, theodolites were large and relatively simple in construction. Today they are small and complex but easier to use, as you will find out later. By the way,

the actual ground mark for pillar stations is usually about 4 feet below the ground.

Why is it below the ground?
To protect it. A great deal of time, effort and cost was involved in fixing the exact position of these points on the Earth's surface. The pillar marks the location and, as we have already seen, does away with the need to use a tripod on which to hold the theodolite in these often windy locations.

Set into one side of the pillar was a metal plate to which Mr. Cameron drew the boys' attention.
"This is a Bench Mark; it marks a point of known height above sea level," he said. **"There are nearly 750,000 of these and you'll find them cut on buildings, bridges and walls close to roads, as well as on these pillars."**

One of the Cubs pointed to a number on the plate and asked: *"Is this the height?"*
No, it's the reference number of the Bench Mark.

What do you mean by height above sea level? The level of the sea goes up and down with the tide!
It also varies from place to place! Our 'datum' point — that means reference point — is related to the mean sea level at Newlyn in Cornwall.

What's mean sea level?
It's the half way point between the highest high tide and the lowest low tide. Now let's see some of our modern equipment.

We walked down the hill and across a lawn to an instrument mounted on a tripod. The boys gathered round to get a closer look, as Mr. Cameron explained . . .

The boys listening carefully as Mr. Cameron tells them about the Bench Mark on the side of the pillar.

With the help of Mr. Peter Ingham (a surveyor in the Information Branch), Mr. Cameron described the workings of the theodolite with a Geodimeter mounted on top.

Simon taking a distance measurement

This grey instrument is the theodolite, and the box on the top is a Geodimeter...

What's a Geodimeter?
It measures distances electronically. It sends out a beam of light to prisms held on a tripod or a pole. The light beam is reflected back to the Geodimeter: we know that light travels at 186,000 miles a second, and a computer in the Geodimeter measures the time taken for the light to travel to the prisms and back, converts this into a distance measurement, and displays the 'answer' on the screen at the back.

How accurate is it?
Very accurate. It gives the distance to the nearest millimetre.

How much does it cost?
This one costs about £8,000 but others able to measure longer distances cost more.

Does it measure distances in feet or metres?
Metres. Ordnance Survey has measured in metres since the late 1940s. We can easily convert back to miles, yards, feet and inches, if necessary.

As the Cubs made their way back to the main building Mr. Cameron explained that, wherever possible, aerial photography is used to help O.S. surveyors. The O.S. takes aerial photographs between March and October. It hires aircraft and flying crews, but uses its own cameras and operators. An aeroplane flies over the ground at a constant height along a series of straight 'paths'. The photographs are taken at regular intervals so that each overlaps the next one by 60% on the same path and 25% with the photographs on the 'paths' either side.

Since the 1960s the Ordnance Survey has used computer technology to help its surveyors and draughtsmen with survey calculations, area measurement and map production. "It is a bit complicated," Mr. Cameron said, "but at least you'll be able to *see* what happens.'

For the next hour or so, the boys visited various areas of the complex, and discovered that there was more than one way of preparing a map for printing. They were amazed at the amount of skill and work that is needed.

In one huge room they saw many plotting machines. Ron Levett showed them how a Zeiss Planicart stereo plotting machine worked. A pair of aerial photographs are placed in the machine. The operator looks through the machine's binoculars and sees a small black dot and a three-dimensional picture of the ground. Using his two eyes, two hands and two feet, he traces the dot over every feature he sees and a linked 'pen' draws out his trace on the attached plotting table. The operator can also survey the contour lines by setting the dot at the required height, then tracing round the landscape.

"Can this machine make the whole map?" one of the boys asked.

"No," replied Mr. Cameron. "Trees and shadows hide map features and you can't see the names of roads and farms or house numbers on the photographs! These traces, now called 'Master Survey Drawings', are always passed to our field surveyors to complete."

The boys moved on to look at one of the most advanced large scale map 'drawing' methods, known as 'digital mapping'. Information which appears in graphic form on the surveyors' completed Master Survey Drawings is converted by electronic means into digital form on magnetic tape. These tapes are then sent to the O.S. Computer Suite.

The Cubs walked through an air lock into a large air-conditioned room. It

The Cubs finding out for themselves how the stereo plotting machine worked under the watchful eye of Mr. Ron Levett.

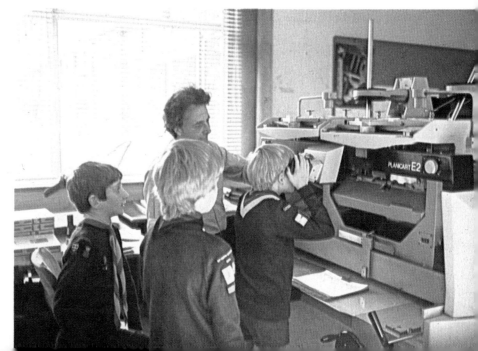

was as if they had passed along a time tunnel into the future. They were wide-eyed with amazement as Gordon Kelly (a Shift Leader in the Computer Operations Room) showed them a machine drawing a map automatically from a reel of magnetic tape. The four ball point pens (with red, blue, green and black ink) raced around the sheet and a map took shape before their very eyes!

How long does it take to produce a map like this?

Well, the pens draw at 40 inches to the second and most maps can be drawn in about half an hour.

Are they special ball point pens?

Yes, because we would have a big problem if one of them ran out. They are filled under high pressure, so each will draw a continuous line more than three miles long. We change them every two days.

Mr. Cameron and the boys examining the map drawn on the air machine plotting table.

Mr. Nigel Maddock telling Mr. Cameron and the Cubs how he digitises a map.

Watching the computer controlled Xynetics plotting machine working.

How are copies of this map made?

Once we are satisfied that we have all the information on this map right, the corrected tape is used with another machine to produce a copy on film and this is used to make a printing plate.

The boys went back through the air lock, but before going down to the photographic and printing works they called into another 'drawing office' to meet Bernadette Martin. She works on small scale mapping which is still 'drawn' using a method called 'scribing'. With a sapphire-tipped tool she was cutting into a sheet of coated plastic which had the map image on it. After she cuts out all the map detail lines it looks like a negative which, together with other documents, eventually goes to produce the printing plate.

In the vast air-conditioned photo and printing works there were cameras as big as houses, and a wide range of proving presses for printing relatively small numbers of copies, and large multi-colour rotary presses for printing long runs.

MAKING A MAP
A `Simplified´ Flow Chart

Measuring to provide a ◄ · · *as necessary* · · ·
'position' framework
(Triangulation Stations)
and
'height' framework ◄ · · *as necessary* · ·
(Bench Marks)

Aerial photography ◄ · · *as necessary* · ·

Plotting from photographs

Map completion on ground ◄ · · · · · · · · ·
(Master Survey Drawing)

Digitising or Scribing as an · · · · · · · ·
alternative

Map on computer tape
(Tape also used to draft some smaller scale maps)

Map on photographic film ◄ · · **Map Revision**

Plate making

Printing

Completed map on paper
and computer tape and
microfilm

Drafting of ─────► Selling
derived small
scale maps

opy of
rveyor's
1250
d
2500 scale
aster Survey
rawings

Mr. Cameron showing the boys a sapphire-tipped scribing tool while draughtsman Mr. Stuart Birse looks on.

Mr. Cameron and the Cubs watching Mrs. Bernadette Martin scribing a small scale map.

The printed map sheets passing through the 4 colour rotary printing press . . .

. . . and coming out of the folding machine where Mr. Paul Thompson is stacking them ready for their covers.

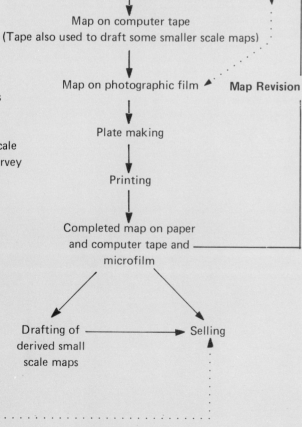

Two of the 'cover sticking' team of ladies putting on the outer covers.

The boys having a go at putting on map covers themselves: (from the left) Mrs. Sandra Davis with Mark, Mrs. Barbara Dedman with Simon and Mrs. Joan Stickland with Richard.

How many maps do you print each year?
About nine million. We sell about 4 million of our own maps each year — the rest are produced for the Ministry of Defence, the Institute of Geological Sciences and other agencies, and we print maps for many overseas countries.

The boys inspected the folding machines and the machines for putting the outer covers on the folded maps. However, when there's a rush on, a team of ladies put the map covers on by hand.

The boys watched, fascinated, as the ladies deftly glued and stuck.

"That looks quite easy!" one of the Cubs remarked.

"Would *you* like to have a go?" came the reply.

The lads didn't need a second invitation. The ladies showed them what to do, and all three then discovered that the task wasn't as easy as it had looked.

On the way back to Mr. Cameron's office, the boys were shown round the permanent Exhibition Centre.
"Is there anything else you'd like to know?" Mr. Cameron asked.

How many people work for Ordnance Survey?
Altogether there are about 3,400.

Do they all work here?
No, about, 2,300 are based here in Southampton. The other 1,000 staff are permanently located throughout the country with local head offices at Edinburgh, Harrogate, Nottingham, Bristol and London. Between them, these offices are responsible for about 180 sub-offices.

Is there always going to be a lot of work for them?
Certainly. If you think about it, O.S. is in the information business, and the information must be up-to-date as well as accurate. Things are always changing, and as long as there is change we will need to be there to measure it, record it and make it available as soon as possible.

It had been a long day during which the boys had learned a lot, and walked for what seemed like miles, and had had a great time.

Mr. Cameron had one last surprise in store for them. He presented each Cub with a personal certificate stating that they had been a surveyor, draughtsman and printer for a day. For the three boys — and for you now — a map means much more than a sheet of paper with printing on it. Oh! and by the way, some O.S. maps (the large scale ones) are also available on computer tape and microfilm!

In the main entrance hall with Mr. Cameron explaining to the Cubs how a theodolite made in 1795 worked.

Mr. Cameron presenting Mark with his special certificate.

What's in a Name?

by Margaret Manson

Illustrated by Martin Aitchison

Do you know the meaning of your name? The present royal family have taken the name of their oldest residence: Windsor. Years ago many people were described by the place where they lived: Richard at the Lea, William by the Green, Thomas at the Ash, John by the Broc's (Badger's) Bank. Later these names were shortened to Atlee, Green, Nash and Brocklebank. Shaw was a grove, Thackeray an area for storing thatch, and Yates lived by a yat or gate.

The first Stuart or Stewart was a steward: his name was derived from the office he held. The steward was the Lord of the Manor's deputy. Under him, Butlers bottled the wine, Napiers had care of the linen, Forsters and Fosters were foresters. Other trades from which names are derived include Coopers, who made barrels and casks; Bolters who sifted flour for the Miller, and Baxters who were female Bakers. Clerks were sometimes called Latiners (which became Latimer). Masons worked in stone; Cartwrights, Wheelwrights and Wainwrights worked with wood.

The Smith worked in metal. In a village he did everything from shoeing a horse to making armour, plates and cups. In a large city like London, the smith became more specialised. The Locksmith became known as Locks, Lockyer or Lockton. The Knifesmith was Naismith or Cuttler. Nailsmiths became the Naylors. When armour was not being dented in war, it was rusting in peace, and the Smiths who repaired it were the Furbishers or Frobishers.

The Plantagenet kings acquired their name from Geoffrey of Anjou's (the father of Henry II) habit of wearing a sprig of broom in his hat. The Latin name for broom is *Planta genista,* which became Plantagenet. In more modern times, when Robert Baden-Powell first wore a broad-brimmed hat in Africa, the local people named him Kantankye: 'The Man of the Big Hat'.

A distinctive garment earned its wearer the name Mantle, and a brightly coloured one, conspicuous among the brown homespuns, acquired a colour name for its owner - Purple, Pink or Scarlet.

A red Welshman among dark neighbours was known as Griffiths. The Rouses, Russells and all the Reeds derive from Red. A very fair complexioned person in a dark community was a Blunt, Blund or Blount from the word blonde, or perhaps Blanchard or Blancheflower from the word blanche.

An easy way to describe people was to compare them with a bird or an animal. One would be as fleet as a Hare, another as cunning as a Fox; others might sing like a Lark, a Linnet or a Nightingale. Those who were alert or who had keen senses of hearing were Hawkins Hawkshead or Hawksworth.

Exceptional strength was noted as Armstrong, and a lame or crooked leg in Cruikshank. Long, Lang and Longshanks meant a tall man, whereas small people were Pettit or Little.

Some names embarrass their owners because the meaning is now obscure. Onions is such a name - it was originally a personal name, Ennion.

So what's in a name? However weird it may seem, we can be certain that every name has a meaning. What does your name mean? Do some research of your own and find out!

CLIFF BROWN'S PUZZLE PAGES:

ANSWERS ON PAGE 63

PAIR UP THE BUTTERFLIES

The buddleia bush attracts all kinds of butterflies. Look carefully at this picture. There are nine pairs of identical butterflies. Can you find them?

DOUBLE-BARRELLED WORDS
Study these twelve pictures and make six double-barrelled words

'DOWN BY THE RIVER' CROSSWORD

Can you complete the crossword using the picture clues? (A=across, D=down)

42

SPOT THE DETAILS

HAVE A GOOD LOOK AT THIS PICTURE OF THE TERRIBLE TYRANNOSAURUS REX, BECAUSE YOU HAVE TO DECIDE WHICH OF THE CIRCLES BELOW ARE ACTUAL DETAILS OF THE PICTURE, AND WHICH ONES HAVE BEEN 'FAKED' BY OUR ARTIST.

A PEBBLE MAZE TO A 'DOT TO DOT' DESTINATION

THIS LAD WILL NEED TO BE CAREFUL CROSSING THE PEBBLES TO GET TO THE WATERSIDE TO CATCH A FINE SPECIMEN OF SOMETHING. FIRST YOU MUST GET HIM TO THE WATER **WITHOUT** CROSSING A BLACK LINE— AND THEN FIND OUT WHAT HE'S AFTER BY JOINING THE DOTS IN NUMERICAL ORDER.

GOOD VIBRATIONS FROM GARBAGE

Simple musical instruments such as those illustrated are ideal for campfires and other occasions — especially if you organise a group and do a little serious rehearsal.

It is amazing just how many musical instruments you can make from odds and ends of scrap. You'll enjoy making them, and playing them, and bringing pleasure to others.

THE PIPES OF PAN

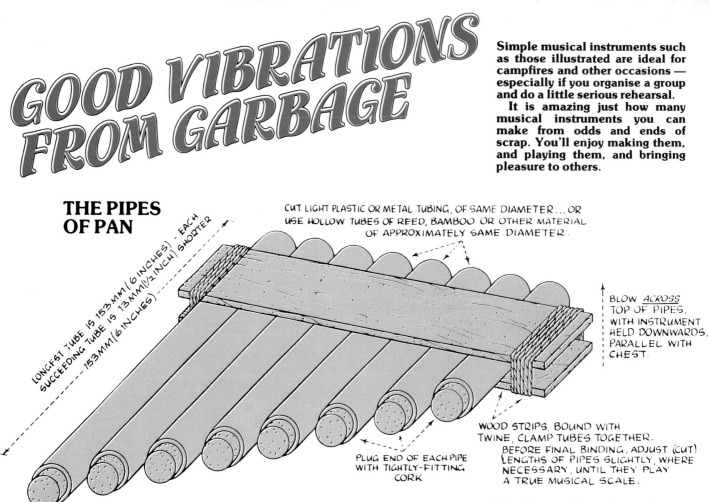

CUT LIGHT PLASTIC OR METAL TUBING, OF SAME DIAMETER ... OR USE HOLLOW TUBES OF REED, BAMBOO OR OTHER MATERIAL OF APPROXIMATELY SAME DIAMETER.

LONGEST TUBE IS 153 MM (6 INCHES) - EACH SUCCEEDING TUBE IS 13MM (½ INCH) SHORTER 153MM (6 INCHES)

BLOW *ACROSS* TOP OF PIPES, WITH INSTRUMENT HELD DOWNWARDS, PARALLEL WITH CHEST.

PLUG END OF EACH PIPE WITH TIGHTLY-FITTING CORK

WOOD STRIPS, BOUND WITH TWINE, CLAMP TUBES TOGETHER. BEFORE FINAL BINDING, ADJUST (CUT) LENGTHS OF PIPES SLIGHTLY, WHERE NECESSARY, UNTIL THEY PLAY A TRUE MUSICAL SCALE.

This instrument is known as Pan's Pipes, or the Syrinx. It was first used thousands of years ago. In Greek mythology Pan was the god of shepherds, huntsmen and rural people, and also the protector of flocks and herds, and of wild beasts, and bees. The ancient Greeks showed Pan as having the body of a man, with two small horns, and the lower limbs of a goat, and they credited him with inventing this musical instrument.

The instrument was originally made of hollow reeds of graduated lengths fastened together in proper order to produce a musical scale. You too can make it from tubes of reed or bamboo — or from scrap plastic or aluminium or other tubing.

The sound is made by blowing **across** the open upper ends, which must be level so that the mouth can pass easily from one tube to another. With practice you can produce excellent music. It is an ideal campfire instrument. Make it as follows:

1. You need 8 hollow tubes, each of a different length — see sketch. Make the longest tube 6 inches (153mm), and the shortest 2½ inches (64mm); this gives you a difference of ½ an inch (13mm) in the length of each of the 8 tubes. The diameter of each tube, or pipe, should be the same.

2. As illustrated, clamp the pipes between two strips of wood. Bind each end of the wood strips with strong twine. Fit a cork into the end of each pipe. By blowing **across** the open upper end, test each pipe for true scale. You will have to experiment a bit, trimming the pipes to the correct lengths, until they play a true scale. The longer the pipe, the deeper the note.

3. Very slight adjustments to the corks can also help achieve true scale. When you have achieved a true musical scale you can further secure the pipes in position by using a suitable strong adhesive to stick the pipes to the wood strips, and to one another. You can also if you wish cut tiny wood blocks to size, and glue them between the wood strips at each end.

MARACAS

Associated with South American music, Maracas come in pairs, being played with one in each hand. Rattling instruments of one kind and another have been known for ages virtually all over the world, and the origins of many are lost in the mists of time. They range from African anklets made from seed pods that rattle as the dancer moves, through to small turtle-shell rattles tied to the knees of dancing priests, as in the Snake Dance of the Hopi Indians of Arizona.

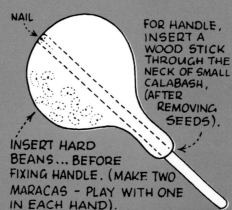

NAIL

FOR HANDLE, INSERT A WOOD STICK THROUGH THE NECK OF SMALL CALABASH, (AFTER REMOVING SEEDS).

INSERT HARD BEANS... BEFORE FIXING HANDLE. (MAKE TWO MARACAS - PLAY WITH ONE IN EACH HAND).

You can make a pair of Maracas from two dried calabash gourds containing dried beans, as illustrated. However, calabash gourds are not generally easy to acquire, and plastic containers such as washing-up liquid bottles or detergent bottles, of a suitable shape can be readily substitued. Tin-can rattles can be made in a similar way.

The sounds of rattles differ greatly, from the sharp to the subtle, according not only to the kind of container you use, but also according to what you put in the container. In the same container, dried beans will make a completely different sound from, say, lentils or rice grains, just as small pebbles will make a different sound from, say, coarse sand.

BOTTLE XYLOPHONE

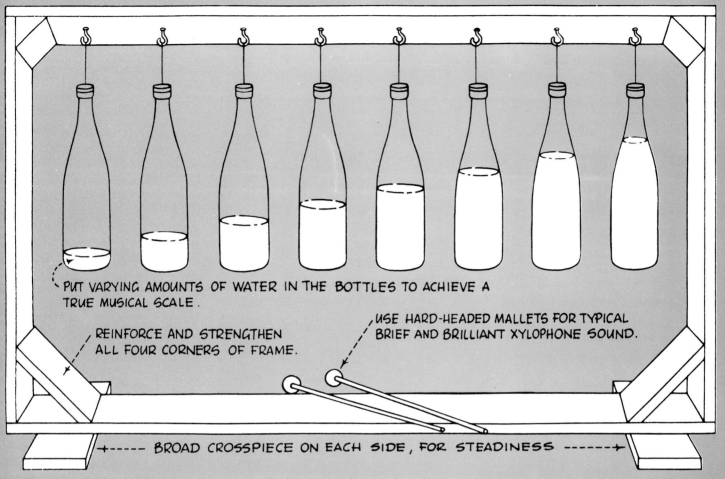

PUT VARYING AMOUNTS OF WATER IN THE BOTTLES TO ACHIEVE A TRUE MUSICAL SCALE.

REINFORCE AND STRENGTHEN ALL FOUR CORNERS OF FRAME.

USE HARD-HEADED MALLETS FOR TYPICAL BRIEF AND BRILLIANT XYLOPHONE SOUND.

BROAD CROSSPIECE ON EACH SIDE, FOR STEADINESS

All the instruments that are played by striking with some sort of mallet or drumstick are called percussion instruments. Some percussion instruments, such as a drum, are used mainly for marking rhythm but others, like the Xylophone, have a scale of notes. Thus, the Bottle Xylophone provides harmony as well as rhythm, and can therefore be a most important instrument.

Collect 8 empty glass bottles; 750ml bottles are excellent. Suspend them in a strong wooden frame built along the lines shown in the sketch. You can hang them from strong string **or** thin wire or you can bore eight notches along the edge of the top board of the frame and suspend the bottles from the notches as indicated in the small sketch. You also need two hard-headed wooden mallets.

When the frame and the bottles are ready, carefully pour water into each of the bottles so that, while the bottle at one end has hardly any water in it, the bottle at the other end is almost full. By striking each bottle with a mallet to produce a musical note, and adding or removing water from each bottle as required, you can soon produce a true musical scale. If you have a piano or other suitable musical instrument handy — even a mouthorgan — you can get the bottle notes in the perfect desired key.

When you've achieved a true musical scale, mark the water level on each bottle with durable paint; in this way you can easily refill at any time to get your notes correct. Once your bottles are tuned, you have a splendid musical instrument that's made from junk and costs you nothing.

ANOTHER WAY OF SUSPENDING YOUR XYLOPHONE BOTTLES... IF YOU HAVE THE TOOLS! THIS CALLS FOR BOTTLES WITH A PRONOUNCED RIM OR BULGE AT THE TOP.

NOTCH

THE SISTRUM

The Sistrum is one of the oldest of all musical instruments. It was played in ancient Egypt, for example, in connection with the worship of Isis, the goddess who was the wife of Osiris and the mother of Horus. Isis was originally the earth goddess and afterwards became the moon goddess. However, this jingling instument was also used by ancient South American peoples such as the Mayas and the Incas. Some researchers have found many parallels between the ancient civilisations of Egypt and South America, and the Sistrum is but one of them. The theory is that a great cataclysm brought about the sinking of Atlantis, once a big continent in the Atlantic Ocean and that some survivors sailed East to Egypt, and some West to South America, taking their knowledge with them.

However that may be, the Sistrum is a most useful instrument and easy to make and to play. The ancient Egyptian version, incidentally, had a metal fork, not a wooden one as shown in the sketch. You'd get a completely different sound, of course, if you decided to be authentic and made your Sistrum from, say, a rod of iron as used for reinforcing concrete, and used metal discs strung on wire across the U-shaped top. You can quite easily bend a piece of iron rod into a U-shape or fork, so that the centre part of the rod is brought together to form a handle.

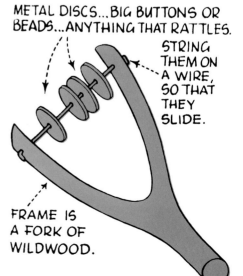

METAL DISCS...BIG BUTTONS OR BEADS...ANYTHING THAT RATTLES.

STRING THEM ON A WIRE, SO THAT THEY SLIDE.

FRAME IS A FORK OF WILDWOOD.

DRUMS...
FOR RHYTHM

The percussion section of your campfire group or band embraces all the instruments that are played by striking with a mallet or drumstick. Cymbals are also a part of this section, being struck one against the other. Especially if your group is used to accompany traditional African or other lively folk dancing, drums and other rhythm instruments will play a big part. In music, rhythm is as important as melody.

The accompanying drawings show you how you can make drums from scrap materials. In the case of the flower-pot drum, earthenware pots are difficult to find these days, and a plastic flower-pot will do — or adapt some other kind of plastic container.

INNER-TUBE DRUMHEAD

TIE WITH CORD UNDER RIM OF POT.

MADE FROM A LARGE CLAY FLOWER (PLANT) POT, THIS DRUM'S INSPIRED BY THE EARTHENWARE DRUMS FOUND IN MANY PARTS OF AFRICA. PLAY IT WITH THE FINGERS, OR WITH DRUMSTICKS.

A SMALL, LIGHT PLASTIC WATER CONTAINER

LIKE THIS... MAKES A FIRST CLASS FINGER-DRUM. SO DOES A LARGE PLASTIC BLEACH BOTTLE!

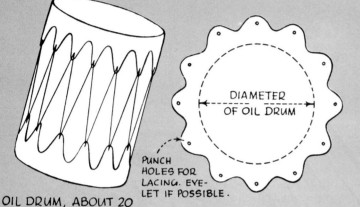

DIAMETER OF OIL DRUM

PUNCH HOLES FOR LACING. EYELET IF POSSIBLE.

OIL DRUM, ABOUT 20 LITRES, WITH ENDS CUT AWAY, AND RUBBER INNER-TUBE DRUMHEADS LACED ON.

CUT DRUMHEAD AS SHOWN ABOVE, ALLOWING ADEQUATE

OVERLAP. SCALLOP OVERLAP BY MARKING 12 EQUIDISTANT POINTS (LIKE A CLOCKFACE) AROUND CIRCUMFERENCE OF OVERLAP. DRAW ON SCALLOP CURVES, AND CUT.

PADDLE RATTLE

The illustration shows you how to make a Paddle Rattle. The paddle should be about the same size as a table-tennis bat, but much thicker — say a centimetre thick — to take the nails. Remove the lining from the crown cork bottle tops, and be sure that the metal bottle tops rattle loosely. To play it, hold the Paddle Rattle in one hand, and tap it against the other hand, in rhythmn with the music.

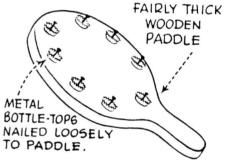

FAIRLY THICK WOODEN PADDLE

METAL BOTTLE-TOPS NAILED LOOSELY TO PADDLE.

SAND BLOCKS

MAKE TWO "SAND BLOCKS" LIKE THIS.

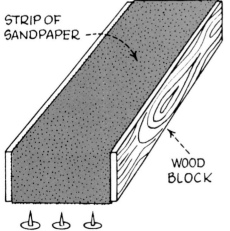

STRIP OF SANDPAPER

WOOD BLOCK

USE DRAWING PINS TO FASTEN SANDPAPER TO WOOD BLOCK, AT EACH END.

You need a pair of Sand Blocks. You get a most pleasant "shuffle" rhythm when you hold a Sand Block in each hand, and brush them gently together. As the illustration shows, a Sand Block consists simply of two pieces of wood, covered with a strip of fairly coarse sandpaper. If you are going on an extended camp, take along a few spare strips of sandpaper.

The sketch gives you the main details. The kind of paper you use is important — you need a piece of thin, **hard** tissue paper that will vibrate effectively; experiment with different kinds of tissue paper.

You do not blow into a Kazoo — you **hum** into it. The Kazoo is a most effective campfire instrument, and you can have a lot of Kazoo players in a campfire group or band.

THE KAZOO

HUM INTO KAZOO AT THIS END

SMALL HOLE

PAPER HELD ON WITH RUBBER BAND

CARDBOARD TUBE

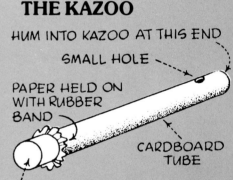

STRETCH WAX, OR TISSUE PAPER OVER ONE END OF A CARDBOARD TUBE ABOUT 4cm (1½") DIAMETER. HOLD PAPER IN PLACE WITH A RUBBER BAND. MAKE A HOLE ABOUT 6mm (¼") DIAMETER, APPROXIMATELY 3cm (1¼") IN FROM OTHER END.

THE WASHBOARD

WHISTLE, BICYCLE BELL AND HORN, FOR COMIC SOUND EFFECTS.

TO PLAY A WASH-BOARD, YOU WEAR A THIMBLE ON EACH FINGER OF ONE HAND.

The pioneers of old, living in rough and often remote conditions, had no radio or television and had to create their own amusements and make their own music from the limited resources on hand. The Washboard is an excellent example of this.

Played with thimbles on the fingers, it is a useful rhythm instrument. The thimbles are brushed across the small corrugations, and can also be tapped in drum fashion for another effect. You don't necessarily have to have the other items shown in the sketch to give you an idea of what the oldtime Washboard looked like with its bicycle horn, bicycle bell and whistle attachments. If you cannot locate a second-hand Washboard, you can make one yourself from any suitable piece of corrugated metal or plastic sheet.

BULL FIDDLE

In the old pioneer days the Bull Fiddle was invariably made from a wooden tea-box. These are hard to find today, but if you cannot get hold of a tea-box you'll find a small metal drum — about 20 litres or more — very effective. In fact the old-timers sometimes used an old galvanised iron bucket, and the Bull Fiddle was also known as the Bucket Bass. The sketch shows you how to make a Bull Fiddle.

To play the Bull Fiddle, put one foot on top of the drum, and place the notched piece of old broomstick on the ridge of the drum. Your one hand, usually the left, holds the broomstick near the top, moving the broomstick to put pressure on the string, while you pluck the string with the thumb and fingers of the right hand. Deep humming notes are produced, which vary according to the tension you place on the string through the degree of pressure on the broomstick. An expert can produce some wonderful music on a Bull Fiddle which — like the Double Bass in an orchestra — has a gruff, heavy tone that provides a firm background for the melodies of other instruments.

HOLE

BROOMSTICK, ABOUT 1 METRE (3' 6") LONG, SLOTTED AT END TO FIT RIM OF OIL DRUM.

HEAVY DOUBLE BASS STRING FROM MUSIC SHOP, OR PLAITED NYLON STRING OR NYLON FISHING LINE ... THREADED THROUGH 6mm (¼") DIAMETER HOLE BORED NEAR TOP OF BROOMSTICK.

STRING THREADED THROUGH 6mm (¼") HOLE IN CENTRE OF BOTTOM OF OIL DRUM ... ANCHORED INSIDE BY TYING TO 1cm (½") DIAMETER WOOD DOWEL.

NOTCH, TO FIT RIM.

20-LITRE (OR LARGER) OIL DRUM.

Cartoon by Peter Harrison

The Story of Rope

Words by Eric Franklin

Illustrated by Peter Harrison

The story of rope is closely tied up with the story of man! Rope was undoubtedly one of man's earliest tools, and possibly one of his earliest weapons. By the late Stone Age man had discovered how to twist plant fibres into cords and ropes, and to make nets.

History and legend have many references to rope and to knots. The Ancient Egyptians were skilled rope-makers: when the Great Pyramid was built during the reign of King Cheops about 6,000 years ago, ropes were used to haul the huge blocks into position. A model of a fully-rigged ship with an abundance of ropes and knots was found in the tomb of Tutankhamun. When Xerxes with his army crossed into Europe he employed Phoenicians and Egyptians to make the ropes that held together the bridge of boats he built across the Hellespont.

When Gordius, a common man, became King of Phrygia, he tied his cart to the temple pillars with a knot which no one could untie. An oracle then proclaimed that whoever could undo this knot would rule the world. No one succeeded until Alexander the Great who, exasperated by his inability to untie it, drew his sword and sliced it in two. Later, he did become ruler of most of the then known world. In Ancient Greece the Reef Knot was known as the Hercules Knot, since that hero was supposed to have invented it.

Right from the beginning of Scouting, ropes and knots have been associated with Cub Scouts and Scouts. Baden-Powell wrote in his book *Scouting For Boys:* "Every Scout ought to be able to tie knots," and then described and illustrated eight knots which he felt we should all know. With a good knowledge of knots a Cub Scout or a Scout is prepared for a number of emergencies, including the possibility of saving life, as well as possessing knowledge of great value in many circumstances.

So, early in our existence as Cub Scouts, we are introduced to ropes and to the tying of knots, and rope seems to be quite commonplace stuff which we take for granted. But how many of us know how ropes are made and what they are made of?

To find out we took some Cub Scouts to a works of British Ropes Ltd in South East London, through the courtesy of Mr Manners, the Works Manager. There we saw ropes made from natural fibres such as sisal and manilla, and ropes made from man-made fibres such as nylon, polyester and polypropylene. There were cords as thin as a millimetre or two right up to ropes of 144 mm diameter (457 mm circumference). While the 144 mm monster was the largest we saw, we learnt that even bigger ropes are regularly made for the Royal Navy and for merchant ships. We also learnt that British Ropes was founded in 1924 by the combination of several smaller firms and today is one of the world's major rope makers, with factories in fifteen different locations in Great Britain as well as a group in Europe, and with world-wide connections.

Words cannot really describe what we saw so now let the pictures tell you the rest of the story.

Rope making begins by forming strands. The bobbins of rope-yarn are set up on the bobbin banks, from which the yarn can be drawn off into the strand.

The rope-yarns are fed through a reeve plate into the stranding machine. The reeve plate draws together and correctly positions the yarn.

The strand is then drawn through a tight die which compacts and forms all the rope-yarns into a smooth, even strand.

This is a squareline (8 strand plaited) rope-making machine. This construction of rope was first produced for ships' mooring ropes about 20 years ago. The main advantage over 3 strand ropes is that it is unkinkable, and is very commonly used for marine mooring ropes.

The Cubs looking round the store where coils of rope are held between production and despatch.

Photographs by
Harold Wyld

The boys (with Eric Franklin) examining a Braidline (Double Braided) Nylon rope, which was introduced about 10 years ago and is the newest construction for man-made-fibre ropes. The main advantages of this type of construction are great strength, extreme flexibility, lower extension and harder wear.

The squareline rope store holds the coils of ships' mooring ropes waiting to be cut and spliced.

In the Splicing Department the Cubs were shown how to splice the Squareline ships' mooring ropes. The method is very much the same as Scouts learn when splicing 3-strand ropes.

In the Specialist Rigging Department large Braidline nylon ropes are made into Single Point Mooring ropes. The ropes are used to moor tankers to buoys carrying out the transfer of oil from offshore oil wells. These assemblies are produced from the largest and strongest ropes manufactured anywhere in the world.

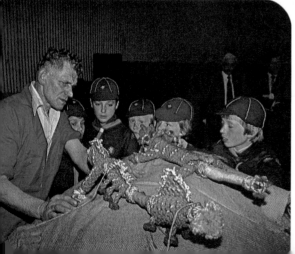

The Cubs rounded off their visit by examining some rope work animals. This type of fancy rope work using a variety of knots was one of the ways old seamen spent their time in the days of sailing ships. They would make bell ropes, sea chest handles, etc. The modern equivalent which anyone can do on a smaller scale is called Macrame.

THE CUB SCOUT ANNUAL *gratefully acknowledges the help and co-operation of Bridon Fibres and Plastics Limited in the preparation of this feature.*

Photograph by David Stower

A VERY SPECIAL BOOK

THE INTERNATIONAL CUB SCOUT BOOK
Published by World International Publishing Limited

If you look at the competition entry form on page 61, you'll see that we ask you to list the three items which you most enjoyed in the Annual. We also invite you to give us a couple of suggestions for features in future Annuals.

We've done this for a number of years, and we do take your suggestions seriously . . . very seriously. After all, you are a very important person because, if we filled these pages with a lot of things you didn't like, you (or Mum or Dad or *someone*) wouldn't buy the Annual next year . . . and that wouldn't do anyone any good!

The suggestions which cropped up time and again were: 'all about Cub Scouts', 'Cubs in other countries', 'more about Baden-Powell', 'the Promise and the Law', 'things Cub Scouts do'. As there is a limit to how much we can put in any one CUB SCOUT ANNUAL (and you like crosswords, puzzles, competitions, how to make things, stories, 'special' features, etc. as well) and, because you are a Cub for only three years, we began to think that maybe you would like a special book which included this sort of information . . . and probably Cubs in other countries would be equally interested.

After some more research it seemed that boys like you were asking such questions as: What was the man who started Scouting like as a boy and a man? What sort of family did he come from? How did Scouting actually start? What were the first Cubs like? How did Scouting spread to other countries? In which countries are there Cubs and Scouts? Just what do Cub Scouts do? And so on.

For over a year we thought and planned and discussed. It was our job to try and find the answers to your questions and to present them in an exciting way which would reflect the adventure of Cub Scouting as it really is. We collected information, ideas and illustrations. It was rather like gathering the pieces of a jigsaw . . . and a very large jigsaw it turned out

to be! Slowly but surely the pieces began to fit together and an overall picture began to emerge. It was a fantastic piece of teamwork, as so many people did so much to help. Here are just a few examples of what I mean.

. . . The World Scout Bureau in Geneva provided a huge amount of material especially for the International Section. They wrote to every Scout Association in the world (there are almost 120 of them) asking for information, photographs and badges. Soon small packets, large envelopes and even parcels containing all sorts of badges, pictures, leaflets and handbooks, etc. flooded into my home. It certainly proved that the

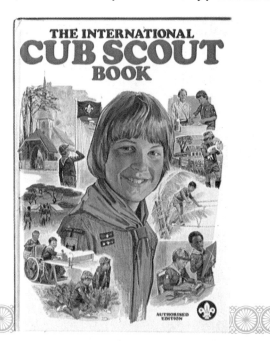

world-wide Brotherhood of Scouting is for real! I must admit that I was a little worried when the badges arrived from Japan as all the labels were printed in Japanese: however, a letter to the Boy Scouts of Nippon in Tokyo soon solved that problem with an English translation . . .

. . . When we couldn't locate a picture of an Australian Cub with their special bush hat, the Queensland Branch of The Scout Association of Australia took a photograph especially for us . . .

. . . The information about Scouting on Stamps came from a gentleman in Rome, Italy . . .

. . . The Boy Scouts of South Africa let us use a map of Mafeking which B.-P. had sketched in 1903, and their Medical Advisory Committee checked the information on First Aid and Emergencies . . .

We also received a lot of help from many individuals and organisations with no direct links with Scouting.

. . . The Museum in Mafeking sent us a set of photographs taken during the Siege of Mafeking 1899 and 1900 (by the way, you can see a number of these pictures elsewhere in this Annual) . . .

. . . Ordnance Survey gave us a copy of a 1906 map of Brownsea Island so we could get an exact idea of what the

What's in the Book?

PART ONE tells Robert Baden-Powell's life story from his birth to the time the Wolf Cub Section was started in 1916. It includes information about his family, his childhood, his schooldays and his extraordinary military career. The first Scout Camp on Brownsea Island in 1907 is reconstructed in words, maps, photographs and pictures. The pages about the early days of Cubbing include a brief biography of Rudyard Kipling, a colourful feature about some of the characters from *The Jungle Book*, and an idea of what the first Cub training programme was like.

PART TWO describes how boys can become Cub Scouts, and gives information about The Promise and the Law, uniform, the Grand Howl and the Investiture Ceremony.

PART THREE (which makes up more than half the book) gives an idea of just how many things Cub Scouts do. It has the sub-title 'A Cub Scout

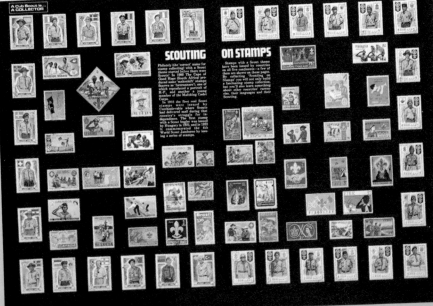

island was like when the first Scout Camp was held there in 1907 . . .

. . . Frederick Warne (the publishers) allowed us to reproduce more than 100 flags from their book *Flags of the World* so that, in the International Section of our book, we could show the national flag of every country in which there are Scouts . . .

. . . Ladybird Books of Loughborough allowed us to reproduce many of the illustrations from their books . . .

And there were many, many more . . .

Add a team of writers, artists and photographers to all this, and you'll begin to get some idea of just how many people were involved. We've done our best to present a vivid picture of the training, qualities and activities which make Cub Scouting what it is today — exciting, adventurous, purposeful and fun.

We reckon that THE INTERNATIONAL CUB SCOUT BOOK is a book for all Cubs everywhere to read, to use and to enjoy. After all, it really was you (or Cub Scouts very much like you a couple of years ago) who gave us the idea in the first place. Who knows? The suggestions you make on this year's CUB SCOUT ANNUAL Competition Entry Form might give us an idea for another book . . .

is . . .' and is packed with information and ideas. A Cub Scout is . . . an observer, a reporter, an investigator, an explorer, a map reader, a sportsman, a pioneer, an estimator, a tracker, a camper, a cook, a surveyor, a collector, a signaller, an entertainer, a naturalist and a conservationist. Quite a list! But that's what Cub Scouting is all about, isn't it? And we haven't forgotten to include something about a Cub's many qualities — he's healthy, prepared, thoughtful, creative, cheerful, helpful, courageous and kind and friendly.

PART FOUR gives a glimpse of the World-wide Brotherhood of Scouting. The International Section lists every country in which there are Scouts. Each country's entry had its national flag, Scout emblems, Motto, Section names and age ranges and the major languages used. More than 25 colour photographs show Scout activities around the world.

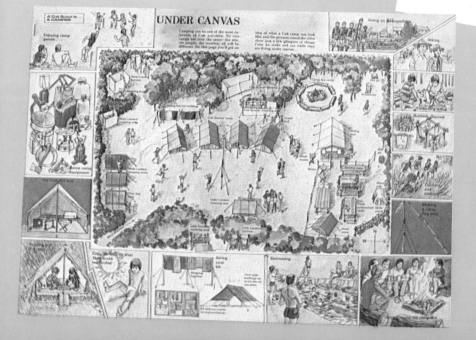

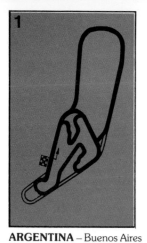

ARGENTINA – Buenos Aires

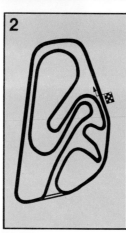

BRAZIL – Interlagos

Grand Prix

On these pages you can see the major Grand Prix Racing Circuits of the World. Look at an atlas and try and find the exact location of each circuit in the particular country.

Each year Racing Teams compete in about 18 countries for the World Championship — it's a long

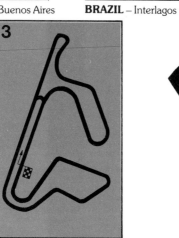

BRAZIL – Rio de Janeiro

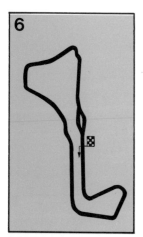

SOUTH AFRICA – Kyalami

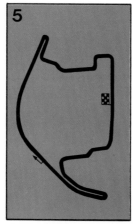

U.S.A. (West) – Long Beach

SPAIN – Jarama

9

SWEDEN – Anderstorp

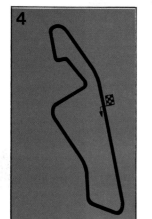

BELGIUM – Zolder

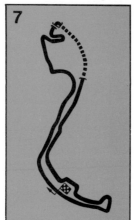

MONACO

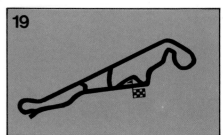

FRANCE – Paul Ricard

Racing Circuits

season, running from January to October or November. Some countries like Britain have two racing circuits which are used alternately. You could use these plans to note the date and winner of each race during 1982.

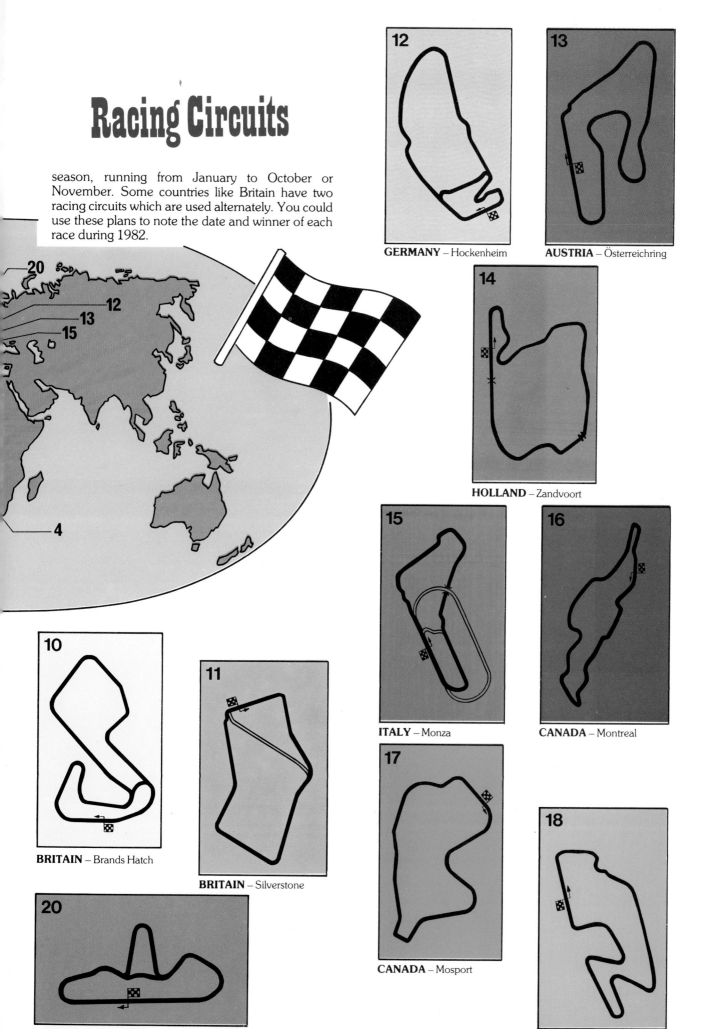

12

GERMANY – Hockenheim

13

AUSTRIA – Österreichring

14

HOLLAND – Zandvoort

15

ITALY – Monza

16

CANADA – Montreal

17

CANADA – Mosport

18

U.S.A. (East) – Watkins Glen

10

BRITAIN – Brands Hatch

11

BRITAIN – Silverstone

20

FRANCE – Dijon–Prenois

SPORTS QUIZ

There are 13 sports illustrated on this page. Can you link each *lettered* piece of equipment with a *numbered* object . . . and name the sport?

Illustrated by Malcolm Turner

Check your answers on page 63

The 1982 Cub Scout Annual KITE

written and illustrated by Bill Bruce

You will need the following materials:

1. Two pieces of wooden dowel, 5mm diameter and 1 metre long
2. Some strong twine or string
3. A tube of quick drying glue
4. A sharp knife
5. A felt pen
6. A ruler
7. Pinking shears
8. A few pins
9. A needle and some strong cotton
10. One brass curtain ring
11. 60 metres of nylon line on a reel
12. Bright coloured paints or pens
13. An old sheet or other material

You won't need many materials to make your own Cub Scout Annual kite, but you will need a large flat area on which to work as you will be doing quite a bit of cutting and glueing.

Cartoon by
Peter Harrison

The Frame

Lash the two pieces of dowel together with strong string or twine and secure the join with some quick-drying glue.

Make small notches about 5mm deep at the ends of each spar with your sharp knife, taking care not to slip and cut yourself. Run some twine or string around the framework, passing the string through the notches and binding the ends tightly. To keep the ends secure, add a few drops of glue.

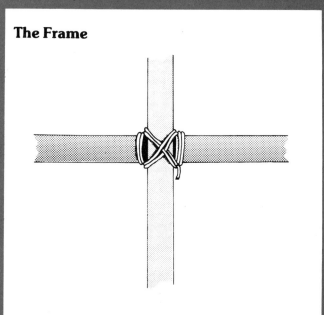

At the base of the kite, take the ends of the twine and form a loop. You will use this later for **attaching the tail of the kite.**

You should now see your kite taking shape. Check that the strings which form the 'diamond' shape are as tight as possible.

Covering your Kite

You need a piece of material that is a little bigger than the frame. Ask your mother if she has an old nylon or cotton sheet or similar material that she no longer wants.

Place the frame on the material and mark around it with a felt pen. With a ruler, mark another line about 10 cms away from the first. Use pinking shears to cut around this line and remove the surplus material.

Fold the edges of the material over the tight string, pinning it at intervals to hold it in position before sewing it together. Ask your mother to help you or to show you how to sew the material together so that it stays tightly on the frame.

Tails

To balance the kite in the air, it will need a tail. This can be made from the off-cuts of material that you used for the main kite.

Good tails are usually about seven times as long as the spine of the kite, so you will need a piece of strong twine about seven metres long and enough pieces of material to attach to it.

It is best to make the tail too long at first, so that if it is too heavy when you try to fly the kite it can be shortened.

The purpose of the tail is to create 'drag' while the kite is flying, helping the kite to fly into the wind. It also acts as a stabilizer and will stop your kite from being tossed around by sudden gusts of strong wind.

This is a good time to decorate your kite before adding the tail and the bridle. You can design all sorts of patterns and pictures and you should find that many different sorts of paints and pens work well. Make your design bold and bright so that it can be seen easily from the ground when it is flying.

The Bridle and Control Line

The bridle is used to attach the kite to the control line and is a piece of strong string or nylon line 1.5 metres long.

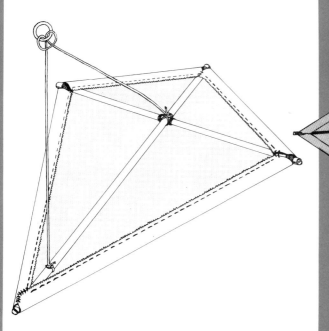

Tie one end of the bridle tightly to the centre of the cross-piece of the frame. Run the bridle through the brass curtain ring to form a 'dove' knot and then take the other end of the bridle to the base of the kite. Tie this end to a point 15 cms away from the base. Secure the knots with a few drops of glue.

The control line will be attached to the brass ring which is known as the towing point.

You will need about 60 metres of strong line such as fishing line or nylon cord. If you are buying line you should ask for it to have a breaking strain of about 5kg. You will need to keep your line on a reel, which you can make quite easily, but if you buy your control line you may be lucky enough to get a reel with it. Tie the end of the control line firmly to the brass ring at the towing point and your kite is ready for its first test flight . . .

FLYING YOUR KITE

Flying a kite is not always as easy as it looks, so do not worry if your first attempts end in failure.

Where to Fly your Kite

The best places to fly kites are large, open spaces like parks, playing fields, beaches and commons. The best launching sites are open to the wind and are well away from trees, tall buildings and overhead power lines. You must never fly your kite within 5km of an airfield or airport and it is illegal to fly a kite higher than 60 metres (vertically).

Launching your Kite

Before you launch your kite, check that everything is secure and that your line is not tangled. Check the balance of the kite before launching, by letting out a little of the line and throwing the kite into the air. If it hangs down on one side you can correct the balance using pieces of Plasticine.

Estimate the strength and speed of the wind and adjust the towing point on the bridle so that the surface of the kite will catch the wind properly. If there is a strong wind, move the towing point towards the front of the kite. This will change the angle of attack so that less of the sail catches the wind. In light breezes, move the towing point closer to the rear of the kite to increase the angle of attack. It will fly better because the wind can catch more of the sail surface.

To launch your kite, hold it at arms-length and away from the direction of the wind. Gently raise your arm and the wind should lift the kite out of your hand.

If the wind is not very strong, you may have to throw the kite into the air and jerk on the line so that it catches the wind. A series of short, sharp jerks should make it rise steadily. As soon as your kite is flying freely let out more of the line.

You may have to practise launching your kite many times before you find the best method.

Landing your Kite

Landing your kite can often be more difficult than launching it. The line of a kite can burn your hands so it is a good idea to wear gloves.

To land your kite, begin by winding in any slack line. In a strong breeze it is easier to do this by walking towards the kite and reeling in the line slowly and steadily.

Using this method, it is possible to get the kite to come directly into your hand without it touching the ground.

In light breezes, bring your kite to within a few feet of the ground and then let go of the slack line. The kite should float gently to the ground. Never drag your kite along the ground once it has landed as this is sure to result in some sort of damage.

WHAT KNOT?

The late Sir Alan Herbert was a great lover of sailing, of the sea and, perhaps most of all, the River Thames. He was an author, poet and one time Member of Parliament. One wonderful poem he wrote was called *The Bowline*. There are several verses but the last verse names a number of knots . . .

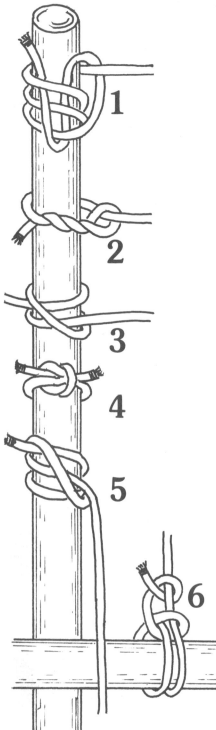

The sailor's knots have qualities he'd
welcome in a bride —
Hold firm when they are wanted, yet are
easily untied;
The more the strain you put on them, the
tighter they do stick;
They are fastened in a flash, but you can
cast them off as quick.
The Timber Hitch, the Reef Knot, the Sheet
and Fisherman's Bends,
The Clove, the sweet and simple hitch on
which so much depends
Have a special duty which they do perfectly
discharge
(Much more than you can say of men or
matters, by and large).
All seamen in their memories preserve a
secret niche
For the nameless benefactor who
conceived the Rolling Hitch,
While manly tears invade my eyes with
which I can't contend
When I discuss the Blackwall Hitch or
Topsail Halyard Bend.
But the Bowline is the King of Knots, and it
is grand to say —
Here is a thing that never will be done
another way.

There are nine knots named and they are all illustrated here. Can you identify them? You will have learnt some of them as Cub Scouts, but the others you will have to search for by asking knowledgeable people or by looking in knot books. There is one which is solely a sailor's knot.

By correctly naming all nine you could win a fabulous prize — the rules of the competition and the entry form are on the opposite page.

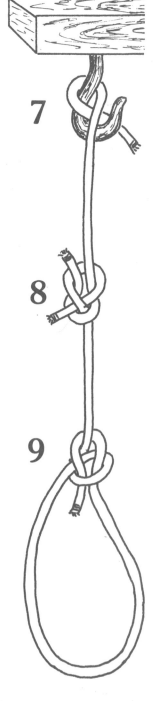

With acknowledgements to the late Sir Alan Herbert,
to the proprietors of 'Punch' and to Messrs Methuens Ltd.

CASH PRIZES

FIRST PRIZE £50
SECOND PRIZE £25
THIRD PRIZE £10

10 Runner-up prizes of a copy of
THE INTERNATIONAL CUB SCOUT BOOK

What it's all about

This year we've set you a knotty problem to solve! If yours is the first correct entry out of the bag you will win FIFTY POUNDS! Just think of what you might buy with that extra money!

Here's what you have to do

1. Look at the opposite page. Read the poem carefully and look at the illustrations of the nine knots. All nine knots illustrated are mentioned in the poem, and it's your task to name each knot correctly on the entry form below.
2. Put your answers in BLOCK CAPITALS in the numbered boxes on the entry form. Fill in your name, address, Pack, date of birth and other information requested.
3. Neatly cut out the entry form along the dotted line and send it, to arrive not later than 31st January 1982, to:
CUB SCOUT ANNUAL COMPETITION,
Baden-Powell House,
Queen's Gate,
London,
SW7 5JS.

The rules

1. All competitors must be under the age of 11 years on 31st December 1981.
2. The closing date for the competition is 31st January 1982.
3. The FIRST PRIZE will be awarded to the first correct, complete entry drawn at a date to be arranged in March 1982. The SECOND PRIZE will be awarded to the second correct, complete entry to be drawn, and so on.
4. Prizewinners will be notified by post and the full list of winners will be published in SCOUTING Magazine.
5. No correspondence can be entered into, and entries cannot be returned.

------ cut carefully along this line ------

'WHAT KNOT?' COMPETITION ENTRY FORM

To: Cub Scout Annual Competition, Baden-Powell House, Queen's Gate, London SW7 5JS.
PLEASE COMPLETE THIS FORM IN BLOCK CAPITALS

NAME

ADDRESS

Cub Scout Pack
(if any)

Date of Birth
Please complete this section as well:
The three items I most enjoyed in the 1982 Cub Scout Annual were:

1.

2.

3.

I would like to make these suggestions for features in a future
Cub Scout Annual.

1.

2.

The names of the knots shown
on the opposite page are:

1	
2	
3	
4	
5	
6	
7	
8	
9	

IT'S A CUB'S LIFE!

**Your chance to earn £2 *and* win a
FREE 1984 Cub Scout Annual!**

What's it like to be a Cub? We'd like you to tell us about a particular project, event, incident, activity, etc. which you have enjoyed as a Cub. It can be serious or funny, 'normal' or unusual . . . it's up to you!

All you have to do is tell us about it in not more than 100 words. Send your entry on a POSTCARD (and don't forget your name, address and Pack) to arrive not later than 31st January 1982 to:

It's a Cub's Life,
Cub Scout Annual
Baden-Powell House
Queen's Gate
LONDON
SW7 5JS

We shall select the best ideas for inclusion in a feature in the 1984 Cub Scout Annual.

The writer of each item chosen for publication will receive £2 and a FREE copy of the 1984 Cub Scout Annual.

P.S. We haven't made a mistake! We do mean the 1984 Annual — you see, we really have to be prepared and get everything ready for an Annual a year before you can buy it in the shops . . . so, by the time you read this, the 1983 Annual will be just about ready for printing.

CUBS ARE THE GREATEST!